Praise for *Busy Being Free*

'Compelling, mystical, deeply moving, darkly funny. *Busy Being Free* is a poetic, incisive, uncensored study of female solitude. I adored it'   Dolly Alderton

'A staggering piece of writing: I had to start it again the minute I finished reading it, and it was just as shocking, absorbing and beautiful on rereading'   Nigella Lawson

'Alluring, shocking, welcome and wonderful'
                      Lisa Taddeo, author of THREE WOMEN

'A testament to the power of putting yourself first'
                      Alicia Lansom, REFINERY 29

'A rollicking good read – a lyrical and titillating journey through Los Angeles and North London'
                      Honeysuckle Weeks, *Mail On Sunday*

'Emma Forrest is a master of voicing those human instincts and thoughts which feel too murky or ingrained to be articulated, and yet here she is doing so with enviable elegance on every page'
                      Megan Nolan, author of
                      ACTS OF DESPERATION

'A heart-rending and acerbic memoir of appetite and abstinence'

A THEAT

'The most delicious memoir that kept me in bed all day. I wonder what it is like to live with a mind like Forrest's, which makes such shooting connections between things and sees a great pattern in it all. I think she might be a genius. Eve Babitz didn't die, she just regenerated as Emma Forrest'

Sophie Heawood, author of
THE HUNGOVER GAMES

'Deeply moving and wryly warm'   *HEAT Magazine*

'I've really never read about sex and been so sharply reminded about how much it is tied up with the fundamentals of being a woman. This deep part of ourselves that somehow gets side-lined and subordinated by everything else. This ecstatic voice we so often manage to ignore. I can hear Emma's voice though, and it's woken me up'

Minnie Driver, author of
MANAGING EXPECTATIONS

'As well as being elegantly written, *Busy Being Free* is eminently readable - a treasure trove of profound insights into love, lust and female desire'

Emma Lee Potter, *Daily Mirror*

Busy Being Free

A Lifelong Romantic Is Seduced by Solitude

Emma Forrest

WEIDENFELD & NICOLSON

First published in Great Britain in 2022 by Weidenfeld & Nicolson,
This paperback edition first published in Great Britain in 2023
by Weidenfeld & Nicolson
an imprint of The Orion Publishing Group Ltd
Carmelite House, 50 Victoria Embankment
London EC4Y 0DZ

An Hachette UK Company

1 3 5 7 9 10 8 6 4 2

A CIP catalogue record for this book is
available from the British Library.

ISBN (Mass Market Paperback) 978 1 4746 2064 2
ISBN (eBook) 978 1 4746 2065 9
ISBN (Audio) 978 1 4746 2066 6

Typeset by Input Data Services Ltd, Somerset

Printed in Great Britain by Clays Ltd, Elcograf S.p.A.

www.weidenfeldandnicolson.co.uk
www.orionbooks.co.uk

To Carole Ann. You'd have loved her.

About the author

Born in London, Emma Forrest began her writing career as a teenage columnist on a national newspaper. By thirty, she had published three novels and exited journalism to work in Hollywood as a screenwriter. Her memoir *Your Voice In My Head* is a classic of the genre. Emma wrote and directed her first feature *Untogether*, which premiered at the Tribeca Film festival. Her most recent novel, *Royals*, was the Radio 2 Book Club pick.

Also by Emma Forrest

Royals
Your Voice in My Head
Namedropper
Thin Skin
Cherries in the Snow
Damage Control (editor)

The sky is the colour of blue
You've never even seen
In the eyes of your lover

'Let the River Run'
Carly Simon

Prologue

Not long after my forty-second birthday, my ex-husband puts his arm through mine and tells me about a 21-year-old Brazilian girl he is planning to make his girlfriend. The divorce had finally come through and I was in LA bringing our daughter, CJ, to visit him from London, where she and I now lived. Things had become friendly enough to catch a movie together – just the two of us.

Walking the graffitied Eastside pavements before the film starts, he explains his plan to 'clear the deck' of other girls, as he had once 'cleared the decks' for me. Paula is young, he says, too young (he shakes his head). He wishes she wasn't twenty-one. Having started my writing career as a columnist on a national newspaper when I was a teenager, I feel protective of the very young. Ben feels protective of *me*, both as I was then and as a result of what I was then, since he, too (via the medium of Australian coming-of-age films) was out in the world too early. He also knows what it is to have a minor spritz of fame that isn't worth the cost once the top note of success has burned away. He knows the waiting until middle age to have people pick up on your scent again.

We're both old enough to remember Fleetwood Mac's *Rumours* on vinyl (visceral memories of turning over to the B side, where revelation lives) and young enough that the vinyl was handed down from our mothers. We both have early childhood memories of Abba, though they're different: his a recurring dream of discovering his parents – who were in the midst of a bitter divorce – happily in bed with the four band members. Mine a suspicion, garnered from their videos, that the cheerful bearded men were holding the stricken-looking women against their will.

We arrive at the Vista cinema, to find the manager – having lovingly maintained the theatre's 1920s Egyptian revival columns, ceiling and murals – has dressed up thematically, as he often does on opening weekend. We hired it out for CJ and Ben's joint birthday three years in a row, *Finding Nemo*, then *Singin' in the Rain*, then *Kubo and the Two Strings*. We packed the aisles with friends and family, who were first worrying about the state of our marriage, then looking uncomfortable at how close the event fell to our divorce filing, then, the next year, marvelling at how well we seemed to get on. We were so determined not to divorce the way his parents had.

Some have suggested our friendliness is the reason I fail to countenance dating. It's hard to convince people: I just want to be alone with myself, who I genuinely thought I might never get to see again.

So my ex-husband and I walk, arm in arm, to see *Once Upon a Time in Hollywood*, which is a very long film. In the aisle, he's approached by someone he's worked with, then by a fan, each time introducing me: 'This is my beautiful ex-wife.'

We take our seats in the middle of the row and at first he is delighted by Tarantino's fake trailers. Then, a while into the movie, his leg starts shaking. Then forty minutes before the end, he hisses 'Fuck's sake,' then stands up and barks at the screen: 'Get on with it, Quentin!' And, pushing past all the knees and handbags in our row, past the fan who had approached him, he walks out. I watch him bolt up the dimly lit aisle, as I have watched him turn cars around, take off his wedding ring in a fight, call time, again and again. As I've seen him clutch his face and wail 'No more tricks!' when he opened the cupboard and found Marmite when he'd expected Vegemite.

In the Vista cinema, he is a retreating figure and I freeze, trying to figure out whether to stand up or sit down, thinking how to pick past people who are watching. I'm also thinking how much I'd like to be a man who remonstrates with the screen in packed cinemas or, like the love before, wears pyjamas to the 24-hour supermarket to get ice cream at midnight. Or the boyfriend before that, who, feeling hot, left his new leather jacket behind a bush on his walk to a meeting, then shrugged when, on his return, it was gone. But instead, I've dated them.

Men who have sent love letters from four points of the globe, hand-sewn clothes for me, even though they'd never picked up a needle before, FedExed a T-shirt that stinks of them, enclosed with details of a plane ticket. They've inked beautiful inscriptions to me in the books that meant the most. They've bought jewellery for me. Not Liz Taylor diamonds – my collection is more tactile than that: a corn goddess ring, an onyx heart pendant inlaid with curling gold leaf, a heavy Mexican silver

3

life-size rose brooch. There's a whole novella to be written just about the rings Ben gifted me. There's a different novella about the shelf of Do It Yourself mugs into which he baked love letters when he was still unemployed.

My love for these men dictated everything – the clothes I bought, the trips I took, the work I turned down or flaked on, the cities I moved to. Leaving journalism in my twenties, I had a meeting with a respected Hollywood manager who had travelled to my hotel to talk about breaking me as a screenwriter – and fifteen minutes before our breakfast I cancelled because my boyfriend was flying back to New Zealand that evening and I felt I needed to resolve a fight. She said she understood and I assume what she understood was this: that I was a talented idiot, and that I would always put men above myself and the pursuit of passion above that of career.

Right before I met Ben, I published my first memoir, *Your Voice in My Head*. I was about to marry 'the actor's actor', just as I became, for a certain audience, the suicidal girl's suicidal girl. He's still a great actor, but I am no longer suicidal. I haven't been in years – nor have I self-harmed or been bulimic. I've been on the same meds successfully since my twenties and never had a relapse. But if I meet people who only know me through that book, or travel to countries where it particularly gained notice – Canada, Brazil – they treat me delicately. Which feels confusing. Can you still be gentle with me if you know my struggles are merely domestic, now? Tangible rather than amorphous pain?

The hero of that memoir was my psychiatrist, Dr Rosecan. He died young, but his greatest bequest was not to permit the taking on of mental illness as identity. He gave me my medication but would not give me my diagnosis (I found it in his notes after he passed).

My mantra, when I'm scared, on a turbulent plane, in a faltering relationship or even just to manage feeling overwhelmed by an email is '*I'd like to be myself*'. I don't know how this mantra came about. I just know that she's in there.

I remember, age ten, not understanding why I cried so hard to 'Fast Car' by Tracy Chapman whenever it came on the radio, blissfully unaware that I'd sob to it again thirty years later in the back of a cab, only this time I'd know why. That maybe I'd had my fill of men to run away with. That there would always be a return journey and it would always be alone. That the time had come to travel alone both ways.

Loving other people with all of my heart has not unlocked who I am and what I deserve, and since that hasn't been transferred by osmosis from these bold and admired men – and it hasn't, not by saliva or semen or even by holding hands – now what?

I think, again and again, of the Rilke lines:

> Work of the eyes is done
> Go now and do the heart-work
> On the images imprisoned within you.

Part One

In exchange for being able to live near my family, I signed over my half of our magical mansion on the water. The house of your dreams is something you're meant to work towards, not walk away from. It felt unbearable to leave the mural of Australian animals I'd had painted on her bedroom wall. The front and back garden. The curved lines of the balconies that made it feel you were looking at the mountain lights reflected onto the water from the bow of a ship in motion. It felt unbearable, but it wasn't, because here we are.

I fled London twenty years ago because 1) there was an Oasis video whose plot twist I couldn't understand, so I thought I should really just leave the UK, and 2) not being a drinker had become too oppressive in social situations. My teen years were spent saying 'No, I don't have a drinking problem, I just don't like it.' In a Dumbo drunk elephant bubble of music journalists and bands, it couldn't work.

And because – like a lot of places where people grow up – London is the source of all shame. London was where my 27-year-old crush told the sixteen-year-old me we were good together because we'd always be the least attractive people in any room. Where, the year before that, out among adult journalists, a foreign prince massaged my feet only to expose his penis once the hostess had retreated to her boudoir. I laughed out loud when he told me to put it in my mouth, because how would it fit? He tucked it away and by the standards of men I'd encountered, I thought that it was polite of him to listen.

London, where the cult writer I'd admired who had generously encouraged me to write when I was a thirteen-year-old on my school newspaper, was vicious once I was sixteen with a place on a newspaper. 'Your column,' he hissed to me, 'is as naff as old knickers.' He wasn't wrong, but he also *wasn't asked*. London where the palate-cleansing 'nice' boyfriend I had at seventeen endlessly reported the behaviours of desirable women who turned out to be either 'loose' or imperfect once undressed, as relayed in the office by his friends. The graphic, humiliating, degrading stories the 'nice' boyfriend told about women in the music business haunted me as I understood, years later, was the intention.

London, where, as a very young girl, maybe eleven or twelve, I remember being in my top-floor bedroom, listening, over and over, to the song 'Sweet Harmony' by The Beloved. I didn't know whether or not other kids my age stayed up at night praying not to be alive. Nothing terrible had happened to me yet. But I was alarmed by the world beyond my bedroom. From chocolate Flake ads on TV and *Barely Legal* covers glimpsed in newsagent top shelves, I had the first inklings of what would be expected of me.

I felt haunted by the video for 'The Beloved' single, where the male singer sat in a sea of naked female models, who were lit and posed in a way that suggested their model looks ran secondary to their inner peace. I thought then I could never be as good as any one of those nude, enlightened women. Maybe one of them will read this and tell me how her life ultimately went.

When I lived and worked in Hollywood, I could instantly see things for what they were: you have veneers! You have a trophy wife! You love helping your fellow women! You'll never help your fellow women for fear it may give away that you, yourself, are one. The shape of misogyny was different in the London media world and it took being away to notice it. Living in LA came to an end because the shame of divorce attached itself, like a magnet, to the shame of my youth. And I ended up back at the source.

In this new, old part of the world I left at twenty-one, I can feel my teeth moving at night, shifting with age. I remember that before I left the UK, throughout all of 1998, my mother's primary anxiety – of her myriad and much-admired anxieties – was that leading men's teeth were slipping. I don't remember much about my big screen experience of *The Big Lebowski* and *Out of Sight* except her gasping: 'They're slipping!' – the anxiety was twofold, both for the actors' matinee looks and the likelihood that she'd personally have to catch Jeff Bridges' molars as they showered from the screen (she insisted George Clooney was already wearing dentures).

Marrying Ben was my first real act of disentangling from my parents – about considering how to disentangle, rather than having them ripped from me one day by their death.

But, though we are decidedly middle class, it had not ever been an option for my sister or me to lean on them financially once we left home, to borrow or be paid for, so we never were. When I saw the pilot for the TV series *Girls*, I thought they were like me – bookish Jews – but not like me, because I couldn't fathom parents who paid your rent and how that might affect your path. Marriage to an actor who became successful was the first time I'd ever experienced financial support. It was amazing! I can't recommend highly enough the creative experience of writing a novel without the terror of whether or not all of your bills would be met. It's like being upgraded to business class. It's hard to go back to what you knew before, even though what you knew before was your whole life.

❄

My husband had been waiting all of *his* life to meet the woman who was his mum, if she'd survived. I looked like her. I'd once battled ill mental health, like her. But I made it to the other side and she didn't. I get it now: you want your mum so badly and eventually, you have to leave her. You don't want to leave her, you love her, so you have to be harsh to her in order to make yourself break away. That's part of growing up. I did it to my mum and CJ will do it to me – maybe the divorce has prepped me for what will come.

For a long time, he'd been furious that included in the division of funds were the proceeds of his Sydney flat that he'd bought with the inheritance his mother left him, and which he sold soon after we married. It hurt him very deeply that it counted as shared finances, because his mother died too young and he bought that flat long before he met me. I saw it as inextricably tied to how you choose a wife – to both celebrate and escape from your mother – and that my getting in a divorce half of what she had left behind by dying prematurely was too overwhelming a fusion of the women who had brought him both the most love and the most sorrow.

14

It was sad our biggest stumbling block to getting along was about his mother's flat, because that top-floor flat I took refuge in – that I couldn't have managed the down payment for without *her* proceeds – was integral to my safety.

Though it may be small and lack a garden or air conditioning, once I could tell him to leave my space whenever we short-circuited, and once I could leave his, my whole relationship with him was manageable. As marrying Ben was my first boundary with my parents, buying the flat was my first boundary with him.

Soon enough I had Liberty-print carpet in dusky pink running up the wooden stairs; a Robert Montgomery print high on the place you'd first see as you entered; framed pictures of Elizabeth Taylor, of cats and sometimes of Liz holding cats; and a George Harrison mural in my daughter's bedroom. I had a pink Murano glass chandelier in my bedroom casting sunrise light on the mediaeval lion-and-unicorn wallpaper I'd sourced from Thailand. I bought the chandelier with my first best friend, Eliza, whom I'd met, aged eight, at summer camp. Under the kitchen eaves, I had a miniature Smeg fridge that the previous owners had left behind along with the gigantic views. There was a 1970s Harrods dining table that got hoisted at peril up through the window.

And the pièce de résistance: the spiral staircase I had custom-made to replace the ladder that had sat precariously between the landing and the attic floor. It had cut-out designs in its treads that, like the Murano lamp, cast light across the small space. And it was small – but also, we were so high up, we had gone to the light.

After researching 'bespoke spiral staircases', I explained to the man who would make it: 'Well, I'm a single parent of a small child and she needs to be contained, but can you make it beautiful?' This is the eternal balance not just for a single mother but any parent: can I keep my child safe and still surround myself with beauty? So the steps have patterns cut in them, through which the light can move like stained glass as the day progresses.

Life moves on.

My daughter loved our new living arrangement at first, the closeness necessitated by inhabiting such tight quarters. She didn't mind that – in a neighbourhood with catchment for the state school I wanted her to attend – I wasn't able to afford a flat with a garden. Maybe, like me, she was simply sated that this place, like the one we'd left, had a huge and magical view: where once we looked down on a lake, now we looked up at the stars.

It's both harder and easier to experience plans derailed when you are a single parent. The financial fear is worse. The immersion in adventure is more natural. It's how you – and, I think instinctively, how *they* – keep them believing they're safe.

If your kid feels happy in the new home, in the new/old city, you start to feel like, yes, there's great wells of shame here, but shame could be an exfoliator, to slough off the dead skin of you. I felt a great optimism.

Then, a few months later, I flew my kid back to LA to visit her dad in the 3000-square-foot home in which she'd grown up. We also stayed a weekend with one of my close friends, Shana, who threw CJ a fifth birthday party with a 'real' mermaid in the swimming pool. They are the biggest-hearted family, who happen to have a correspondingly huge home. Back in our little London flat, after we'd dragged our luggage up the flights of stairs, and bathed to shake off the twelve-hour flight, CJ held me by my pyjama lapels.

'What?' I asked. 'What is it?'

Her eyes were *Powerpuff Girl* huge – and she seemed to hover in the air as she slowly stated: 'No more Shana, ever again.'

'But Shana is very kind. Shana and Brian love us.'

She shook my lapels, like a seventies detective who had nabbed their culprit, her voice urgent.

'We are not like them any more. All done. No more them.'

Alone in my room far too late that night – with the view of the heavens and the whole bed to myself – I shook with fear, grief and anger.

All that week, she'd sing the song she remembered from her outdoor nursery school in California, 'Take Me Home, Country Roads' by John Denver. Standing up in her padded raincoat on the top deck of the 102 bus to Golders Green as it navigated roadworks, singing from her deepest lungs and heart:

Blue Ridge Mountains, Shenandoah River . . . Misty taste of moonshine, teardrop in my eye.

And on the worn tartan fabric of the bus seat, I'd dig my nails (that still held the last LA manicure) into the palms of my hands, willing myself not to cry.

A long time ago, when I was still mad and I didn't have a kid, getting manicures wasn't a thing yet and I felt free to cry in public whenever I needed.

If you are a single mother, make sure your kid does not fear they are your romance.

The summer I moved to London, I took my daughter to a Kylie Minogue concert in Edinburgh and, as a reward for a good school report, let her choose what I'd wear. She put me in a fit-and-flare polka-dot dress and black Dolce & Gabbana heels studded with lipsticks. I couldn't explain that I didn't want to wear their clothes any more because they dress the Trump women and so she was dismayed when I wore brown wedges, both PC and wrong with the outfit.

Walking up the cobbled streets to Edinburgh castle, she kept urging me to go back to the room and change so Kylie wouldn't see and have to stop the show.

I tried to deflect: 'The other heels would be too difficult to walk in on cobblestones.'

'You could try! RuPaul could do it.'

Both very tired and aware I was wearing ugly shoes, I snapped: 'I'm not RuPaul! I'm never going to be RuPaul!'

My daughter was only six. After her father and I divorced, she decided to start honing my style for me and, with the concentration of a small child newly entranced by Lego, became determined to build me into a brighter, tighter shape, as if that might somehow draw her dad back. She hid trousers and nixed sensible shoes by saying 'Oh, sorry, too small,' operatically miming a failure to fit them to my foot, like O.J. Simpson trying on the glove in the witness stand.

RuPaul had emerged as her inspiration one day at the bus stop, when we couldn't get her dad on FaceTime. She'd tried to channel her disappointment with the phone by asking that we use it to find 'Pictures of the beautiful black woman'.

'Which one?' I asked.

'The most beautiful one.'

I pulled up Beyoncé, Zoë Kravitz, Lupita N'yong'o, Eartha Kitt. Though, logically, I knew my five-year-old wasn't asking to look at photographs of Eartha Kitt, her unhappiness was about to spill over into rage and I was rifling through the internet as if digging in a cluttered purse for my asthma inhaler.

'The black lady with a boy living inside her!'

'Oh. RuPaul.' Of course.

I suspected she loved Ru so much because he, like her father, is a gigantic personality, who also takes up physical space with his height. Struggling with how to enforce rules as we set up a new home in a new country, I also wondered if she was drawn to the boundaries he sets each week, the calm, confident reprimand he issues his 'children' when they are crossed.

Half of our clothing was still in boxes, but with what we could access, my daughter guided me towards emulating

RuPaul: high heels, hyper-feminine dresses with defined waists. It didn't matter that her dad couldn't see us because he was still in Los Angeles, or that when we were in the same place he could barely look at me, such was his anger about his mum's flat. This was the style she needed me to project in order for the family to reconfigure.

In the end, she surrendered the fantasy of her parents reuniting once she understood RuPaul was a man. Now, she hastens me towards high heels and long lashes so RuPaul will want to marry me, in the manner, I suppose, of two teens in Clash T-shirts drawn to each other as they pass on the street.

As she moved on from agitating for me to get back with her dad, she wanted me to move on, as well: she wanted me to remarry and she wanted to choose to whom. The driver on the bus might have smiled, maybe at me! Or, most viciously, at the Kylie Minogue gig, where Jake Shears from the Scissor Sisters sweetly spent the show dancing and twirling with her while complimenting my pink mohair sweater. When the show ended and we left to go home, she wept and kicked me in the shins.

'We had a great time. Why are you so angry?'

She choked out her accusation: 'You did not marriage the moustache man! *You did not marriage the moustache man!*'

As my daughter was honing her sense of what my style should be post-divorce, I was letting her down by pulling in the opposite direction and wearing a parade of vintage kids' shirts from her closet. I've sourced them at thrift stores worldwide for her but ended up wearing them myself, for the playground and school drop-off, warping the line of *Rugrats*, *Fraggle Rock*, *The Simpsons* with my breasts.

I wore a Ralph Wiggum T-shirt to drop her at her first day of Year 1, knowing the children would find Ralph irresistible. They resisted and I went home realising how unflatteringly the design fell across my bust, for Ralph and for me. Seeing my reflection in a bus window, I saw Amy Poehler – a single-mum character who uses a warm childhood memory as cover for flaunting her hot body and felt a shudder of revulsion I used to feel for adults I'd notice reading *Harry Potter*: this wasn't meant for you. Adulthood changes the shape of things.

Mork & Mindy was the first of her T-shirts I co-opted. She came back from class, pulled it off and, picking up after her, I instinctively put it on my own body, the same way I eat the food she leaves on her plate, the same way I transfer the baby moisturiser from her skin to mine when there's a surplus.

She is still young enough to be in the honeymoon period of her love for me, even more so now it's just us. If I carry her sleeping from a car, she kisses me gently on the lips and breathes 'I love you,' without waking. I'm deep in her subconscious, which makes me feel guilty that I'm also in her wardrobe, warping her T-shirts with my adult body.

Beyond the shared T-shirts and the RuPaul devotion, we also have clothes we match in. This concept of 'twinning' constitutes a whole other psychiatric constellation. Everyone from capitalist behemoths Dolce & Gabbana to fashion-forward brands like Batsheva make mother–daughter clothes.

In my more cynical moments, I think mini-me dressing is for women who don't have their own style, but that's disproven by my friend Maayan Zilberman, a Brooklyn-based artisan sweet-maker who sews her and baby Freddie matching styles. Her own pink ruffled lace blouse was part sacrificed to make a romper, the sleeves now legs, and a banana-print dress gave enough to birth a leotard. I love Maayan's interpretation of sharing clothes with her daughter because it's a metaphor. It says: I would literally give my right arm for you, but I am still me.

But in my own case, I feel that twinning gives off the whiff of parental narcissism, and the possibility that matching outfits both infantilise the mother and pre-sexualise the child. I've leaned into it when I've felt depleted or unattractive. A visual trick – for others, for myself – to convince them that she's adorable, so I must be, too.

Twinning flirts with two worst-case parenting scenarios: that our children shouldn't feel we own them and that our children should never feel confusion about who the grown-up is in the relationship. The boom also returns us to the Middle Ages, when there was no such thing as children's clothing and kids were simply dressed as miniature adults.

Being a parent and now a single parent, I'm examining my boundary issues under a microscope I took from someone else without asking. I didn't gravitate towards wearing my daughter's T-shirts because I think childhood is better or easier than adulthood. My adult life has been less confusing and more rewarding to navigate. One day, my daughter will understand, as I now do, that life can be beautiful and it can also just go awry for a while. She doesn't need to know any of that, not yet. For now, I hug her tight and – as if I am my own RuPaul gently reprimanding myself for transgressing – give her back her T-shirts.

That life can be beautiful and can also just go wrong becomes apparent in early 2020, when, a year after our move to London, the city goes into Covid lockdown.

By moving into that nest of a flat, I had disentangled myself from Ben and my parents.

But I did not want the disentanglement to be because we were literally rather than emotionally incapable of being in the same room. Our untangled branches were held awkwardly at angles, like a child waiting for a high five that never comes. And then pretending they were not awaiting a high five, they were merely measuring the sky.

I wanted to be secure from the chaos of my marriage. I never hoped to be hermetically sealed inside my new serenity by a global death pandemic.

I have two strong past-life indicators of mental health backslide: staying in pyjamas all day and dying or cutting my hair impulsively. As I did both in lockdown, this thought crossed my mind like a lone cloud on a sunny day. These *were* sunny days. Unusually so for London. Because we couldn't go to restaurants any more, I felt like I could taste the colours out of my window, how very sharply delineated the greens of different trees were.

I let my daughter cut my hair – she did a good job, cut dry, a blunt bob at a perfect length they'd never quite got right before in salons. Then, inevitably, I dyed it blue.

The shade I dyed my hair was Blue Moon by Manic Panic. I chose this shade in homage to Kai, a woman who lived across the street ten years ago when I rented a guest house at the top of Laurel Canyon. She had a husband and three beautiful children, each with Crayola hair, and they'd throw parties that would echo through the canyon. She was often in judo whites, which framed both her hair and her exciting mothering style.

I accepted an invite to join one of their gatherings that started in the afternoon and ended past midnight. An impressive Moroccan Jewess with tattooed palms, critical of my drinking abilities, hissed 'God save us from Ashkenazi Jews!'

Though she was a decade older than me, Kai and I became good friends and when my parents visited, she made tea and baked scones for them. As we entered their rustic canyon home, Kai opened the door, wearing her short blue hair, with her teenage daughter showing off her mermaid-green waves. As I tried to introduce them, my mum said:

'I don't understand.'

'What don't you understand?'

'I don't understand. Which of you is the mother and which is the daughter?'

Kai's email address was the top three items on her shopping list because she was always forgetting it – she was too interested in doing judo and dying her hair in the dry canyon sun. Far from that life, deep into lockdown, I held her in my hair, which was more accessible on those interchangeable days than my heart.

I looked OK – if pale – with blue hair but nowhere near as good as Kai, who had deep olive skin. God save us from Ashkenazi Jews. Even now, with the world imploding, I'm still learning the same lesson: how often I forget that I'm not other people. That I can't become the men whose talent I admire by making them fall in love with me nor the women I think are most beautiful by kissing their boyfriends. I can't be the mother who made parenting look like a thrilling lifestyle choice just by using the same hair dye.

Back then, Kai and I were so close that she was at my wedding. She wore a tartan Vivienne Westwood designer dress and her hair was such a rich blue. She said she'd kept the dye in extra long for me. But that was a long time ago. Soon we drifted apart and the last time I tried to reach her, the shopping list email bounced back. Even though it may not exist any more, I still know it off by heart.

By week three of the 2020 lockdown, every retail site I'd ever purchased from had sent me an email saying if we bought from them, they'd be donating 10 per cent or 1 per cent or a kindly thought to our brave first defenders. It repulsed me, or maybe I just felt repulsive. I wore the same thing day after day. I used my clothes to wipe my daughter's nose, so we wouldn't waste any of the precious toilet paper. I drifted in and out of what I eventually understood to be hibernation.

Each evening, my kid pleaded to go to bed and I'd tumble into mine not much later, then wake up and spend my day in the clothes I'd slept in. I was grateful that we'd been, personally, untouched by the tragedy. But, besides that, I was also deeply grateful that I didn't live with a lover, that I didn't have to look OK or – worse – *try* to look OK.

And yet: when we FaceTimed Ben, who had on pyjamas with layers of things underneath them or pyjamas underneath layers of things (it was hard to tell), or reached his elder daughter in Australia – CJ's beloved half-sister Sophia – I'd find myself sad beyond measure. It never occurred to me that, though we're divorced and our family lives on different continents, we wouldn't face the end of the world together. For months before the outbreak, my daughter had been asking what would happen to her if the world ended. 'I would be holding you,' I always replied. But I don't think I completely understood, in my bones, beneath my clothes and my bra, that I would be holding her and that he wouldn't be there in the same frame.

There is a makeshift day bed in the corner of my attic office. I've used it for naps in the past but, in lockdown, I found it both the place where I got the best sleep and the place where I came hardest. When I was awake in it, I'd feel epically sexual. Looking for family films I could stand (to break up her hours of Disney), I showed my daughter *Splash*. When we are meant to be worried Tom Hanks will see Daryl Hannah in the bath with her unfurled tail and discover she's a mermaid, CJ thinks the fear is meant to be that the bath might overflow, which terrifies her. In the 'Papa Don't Preach' video, she is extremely concerned Madonna does not use the hand-rail to exit the Staten Island Ferry. Everything for her is safety concerns and, like the rest of us, she is rarely focused on the right ones. When I was sitting around, worried because we could not afford to buy a place with a garden in her school catchment, I never thought to worry about a human eating a snake that had been bitten by an infected bat.

The rules of Covid-19 are unclear and different to different people, like the rules of marriage. It seemed to mean that only married couples or people who lived together could make love. How could people who are new to each other *not* infect each other? Then again, how could they find each other in the first place?

I found myself feeling sexual about old boyfriends I didn't even particularly want in the first place, about people's dads I'd never seen that way – a biological grab to procreate in a time of human disaster. I wondered how, on the other side of this, I would feel about the possibility, the real possibility, of being with someone again.

And as my mind was full of colour, I was in grey tracksuit bottoms and a top that was a silk-screened numbered edition of 100 and I used to protect with a careful handwash, wringing it out in the sink before laying it flat in the sun to dry so the colours wouldn't drip. But in that first lockdown, I didn't care: I threw it in the washing machine with everything else and was surprised to find it didn't bleed, emerging just fine like a child who can do more than you knew it could, a seven-year-old who can suddenly bathe and put itself to bed. It feels funny to realise I never needed to protect it as delicately as I had, aware, nevertheless, that I might have got something, myself, out of protecting it so diligently.

Clothes, like marriage, are a ritual of safekeeping. Though they may or may not keep you safe, there is pleasure in the ceremony.

In New York, when I was in my early twenties, I thought it was fine to go out in red stilettos, plunge bra, boy shorts and a short silk kimono. That particular evening, I was due to attend the same dinner as a man on whom I was fixated – he was a tattoo artist, a Buddhist, a skateboarder and a chess master. It was like asking Monica Lewinsky (ever-present in the subconscious of Jewish girls of a certain age) to please not fixate on the President. I once timed a drop-in to his parlour so I'd get caught in summer rain, my white top rendered translucent, as planned. The tattooist had precise artistic skill, spirituality and the ability to work the left hemisphere of his brain. Sex, to my 21-year-old self, was osmosis, an act to be engaged in so you wouldn't have to do your own work.

Even today, from my eaves kitchen, I'll hear the clack of four wheels moving fast downhill on pavement and be transported instantly back to New York. What is it about skateboarders that makes them desirable to generation after generation of otherwise reasonable girls and boys? Is it that there is no room on the board for you?

The thing I can see most clearly when I picture New York is my friend Bianca's yellow Marvin Gaye and Diana Ross T-shirt – a pristine vintage find, soon to have ink spilled all over it, which no effort could lift. My despair at this desecration felt out of proportion given it wasn't even mine. Maybe I thought it might be one day (several of Bianca's great finds – including a 1980s Ralph Lauren T-shirt in gossamer peach cotton – ended up in my possession). Maybe I was hoarding any scraps of single-girl despair I could lay my hands on. I remember her tabby cat – he was huge and romantic, so we voiced him as Barry White – and her top-floor walk-up Chinatown flat, her DJ room-mate with the boa constrictor and the rats that would cower in the corner of the snake tank. But mainly, I remember the Marvin and Diana top that cannot be recovered or regenerated.

If you'd asked me what turned me on in bed, I'd have had no idea. I only knew I wanted to be more like the men with whom I sought to sleep. The gap between my appearance and what I actually knew about sex was vast.

As much as I spent on lingerie sets, I couldn't bring myself to pay for toilet paper, preferring to steal it from gallery first nights and restaurant openings. I'd become so friendly with Suzette, who worked the counter at the 'Fresh' cosmetics that had opened on my block, she would do my make-up for these events. Seeing me in my short kimono and red heels through the glass and, with customers hovering, she'd left her post, walked out of the store, and implored me to go back upstairs and get changed. If I had gone back to change, I'd have risked running into the neighbour I'd slept with because his playlist sounded so gorgeous echoing down my chimney. By the time he started playing 'Good Woman' by Cat Power, I'd walked up a flight and knocked on his door. A man with such taste must have something worth transferring. I'd introduced myself and then leaned there, in the doorway, a vampire waiting to be invited inside.

Locked down, I don't wear nightwear outside. Instead I am wearing day clothes to bed: just tracksuits but technically clothes. I think it was a hangover from spending my last decade in California, an extension of keeping slip-on shoes by the bed in case of an earthquake. Not at the beginning, with the man who would become my husband. I wore fifties slips to bed until he was definitely mine, then I wore his tracksuit bottoms and a boy's tank top from Hanes, which remains my alternate sleep look. By then I was in my thirties and I was, under the influence of my future husband's gaze, attracted *to myself*.

I am for other things now.

In my post-divorce London flat, I was amassing two collections: items that, instead of love-bombing someone with, I convinced myself not to post to them and things I agreed to get my kid in order to buy some quiet time. So I had a rare-edition vinyl single 'Theme From Working Girl' by Carly Simon (intended for a man I'd never met who mentioned *one time* in a work email that he loved the film) and a pile of 'LEGO magazine FOR GIRLS'. One day, surely, the two would overlap in my misty single-mum mind and I would scan the news stands seeking 'LEGO magazine for Carly Simons'.

I am used to my thighs touching each other when I walk – this is part of being zaftig, an emotional and physical descendant of Monica Lewinsky. But I had never had before that first lockdown a belly that touched the mattress when I lay down to sleep on my side. I alleviated this by pressing two hot-water bottles and a weighted sensory plush penguin against me at night.

'It does happen in your forties,' said the doctor when I mentioned the weight gain, in the only area I previously could not gain weight if I tried.

I fell back, for decades, on a flat stomach and small waist, because it meant that no matter how much I added to my arse, thighs, hips and breasts, I'd always be a bigger or smaller version of the same shape. I'd always be what I could identify as me, at my core and to my core.

The doctor made a gentle suggestion: 'Everyone is moving less because of the pandemic. You could . . . you could go on a diet?'

But I don't do diets. I eat what I like and walk everywhere. That's the whole point of me. I could, if I wanted, *if I wanted to*, wear a short kimono to an outdoor supper, flip-flops on my feet for the underground and heels in my bag for the arrival. That is, if my sexual drawbridge were down. I mean, who *was* this woman who the doctor suggested would now go on a diet? I, who followed a playlist up a chimney, like a Victorian scamp, looking for love? I didn't know that I could lose weight if I set out to try, because I've never tried. Maybe it felt that way because there were already so many losses: Where was the discontinued grey eye pencil Suzette gave me? The shortie kimono? Where is Suzette herself? The Fresh cosmetics store? The whole New York block as I knew it is now gone. The neighbour I had the affair with after I heard his playlist has a parade of great successes and glamorous girlfriends, says the internet.

'It's OK,' I reiterated calmly on my one mandated lockdown walk a day. 'I have two hot-water bottles and a weighted penguin.'

As a single parent, you can get confused and think: we don't need much space. Just a balcony or maybe a small roof deck is fine. Somewhere I can watch the fireworks from. But London is unprepared for very hot weather and we don't have air con in the attic flat. So locked down, I hauled a paddling pool to the small roof deck, blowing it up when I get there before filling it with water from the hose.

CJ had the best day, paddling as she looked out over the city, from her low-rent infinity pool. And I thought, how cool is this? I have found a way to merge my romantic desires as a writer and her needs as a small child. By romantic desires, I don't mean sex but all the other things that make my heart sing and my soul float.

I tried to hide my face as it dawned on me that eventually, I would need to deflate the pool, which would mean emptying it of water. And I couldn't just pull the plug and let it drain. We were on top of a very high roof, beneath which was my bedroom. In the end, I had to run a hose from the pool, down the wooden ladder, to the bathroom, where I physically and painstakingly used my mouth to suck the pool water out bit by bit, spitting it into the sink. It took an hour. This magic I'd made her wasn't real magic.

It was ungainly and humiliating, and I felt my independent life as a single parent was being mocked by the same universe we'd so blissfully been gazing out on.

Part Two

Our marital home overlooked a tranquil reservoir in LA. At dawn and dusk, it felt like life could be magical. That's two opportunities each day to snap out of yourself – useful for a writer and an actor.

Ben was away filming when I found it and he trusted me to put in an offer without him visiting. It was such a special property, I couldn't understand how it hadn't sold, until I realised the listing had missed out one letter: e. It was listed as a 'modern house', which was why I – no doubt like many others before me – had skipped past it. In fact, it was a 'moderne' house, moderne being the brief but coveted period after art deco, when properties were built with flat roofs and curved exteriors in order to evoke the idea of a ship in motion.

From Frank Lloyd Wright lovers to Richard Neutra nerds, Los Angeles as a city is particularly architecture obsessed – what's still standing after so long carries a powerful aura in earthquake central. These eighty-year-old properties will keep you safe physically, which feeds into psychic safety, two tectonic plates rubbing together.

Stepping inside for the first time, the house was grand, yes, but what I could see through the windows, looking out, was everything. I never dreamed of living somewhere with a view that amazing. It is the thing that kept me afloat. Nobody could enter that home without gasping.

Once the sale of his flat in Sydney came through, we put in an offer.

Los Angeles always felt infinite to me – an endless source of palpable energy. I walked it for so many years, up and down Lookout Mountain, finding film, TV and book ideas with each step. In my formative years in England, I frequently had snowflake ideas that were beautiful, unique and would melt in my hand. In LA, with its seasons of fires, earthquakes and landslides, there was more imperative to write. I had no time for people who mocked this place. I loved LA architecture and fiction, art deco, Dashiell Hammett and John Fante. Walking an unwalkable city, I met men on the hard shoulder of Laurel Canyon Boulevard, where it becomes covered with foliage, who were so feral they looked like the creature behind the parking lot wall in *Mulholland Drive*. Maybe they left me alone because they saw something in me. Maybe they were just surprised to see me. Or maybe they'd been on the streets so long, they didn't see anything any more.

When I first moved to LA in 2005, picking my way up roads with no sidewalks, I didn't know that Ubers would one day exist or that I'd have a husband to give me rides. That I'd meet him in this city and that we'd love and birth and cry and crush each other and be poor together then rich together and sleep in different rooms on different floors, and there would be no discounts, upgrades or recompense, absolutely no complimentary dessert, because there was no manager in our marriage to whom we could complain. I didn't know that my husband would always say, 'Let me drive you.' And when it was over, a facet of the separation was how much he'd resented always driving me. I can understand that. I have also held against men the things that drew me to them, and probably, especially, in the case of my husband.

I did not know I would one day be just a tired mother, pressing 'Walk' at a suburban North London stop sign where everything is designed to suit pedestrians, which, by their very convenience, can make you feel unspecial. As a young, fit person, walking LA's unwalkable streets – I'm a city in a desert! Take me as I am or move home! – the inconvenience was part of the magic.

I moved from New York to Los Angeles following a man. When we got together, he asked, 'Can you try being out here? It will be easier for us.' I should say now: he was married with kids, devoted to his family, there was never any hint of romance between us and yet I eagerly moved coasts at his behest. He just felt like a really good human.

It was a big deal to have caught his attention: he was one of the most successful writers' agents in Hollywood and has become more so in the time I've known him. He was also the anti-sleaze – and I needed that because my life was full of it.

In the years he represented me, I dated a director (he directed me). I dated an actor (he was acting). I dated a fellow screenwriter (he rewrote history). I dated a gifted but troubled comedian who texted late at night:

Hey sexy. What r u doing?

To which I replied:

I'm reading *The New York Times* obituary section.

I was.

I'd discovered the founder of Danone yoghurt died age 103, which is later than the founder of Iyengar Yoga, who passed away at ninety-five. I found this amazing. Still, I put down the newspaper and went over to the comedian's. Because it seemed like I could step inside *The Long Goodbye*? I dyed my hair red because it looked good on olive-toned girls like Sophia Loren and Gina Lollobrigida. But they were much better at being women than I was. This was the last time I was *too young* for a look.

Nobody had seen the films I had seen. Only my parents. You could have affairs with interesting men and try to show them the films you love, but while some of them wanted to see them, as a kind of foreplay, others did not.

I saw the comedian, not because I loved him or thought he loved me, but because I was alone in Hollywood. Every time I ended up at his home, I'd leave a hairslide down the side of the bed, like a prisoner scratching out her days, so that the next new girl in town could find it and know that I had existed.

Of all of those men, do you know who met my mum when she visited me from England? My agent. He was the constant. He knew everything about me, every day. He had even gone round for tea to try to broker a peace between me and the director boyfriend post miserable break-up, so we could keep working together.

Though he doesn't have many years on me, my agent was like a dad, a brother, an old friend. None of these things are meant to happen in an agent–client relationship. Perhaps that's why the end felt so much like a break-up. You know how, in life, either you stay together forever or eventually, you break up. Turns out it's the same with agents. We had only one flaw in our relationship, but it was a doozy: I wasn't making him money; he wasn't making me money.

'It's hard to plug you into the studio system,' he lamented, 'because you're so talented.'

On account of my excess talent, my bills became harder to pay each month.

Because, in Hollywood, nothing ever gets made and love never goes anywhere, I found myself applying operatic pain to non-romantic relationships. My great shining moment came when producer Scott Rudin bought a script of mine for Richard Linklater to direct at Miramax. When, after six months of working with him on it, the Linklater film fell apart, I wandered the pavement-less curves of Laurel Canyon on foot, saying to myself 'No man is ever going to understand me like Richard Linklater did.' It became a mantra:

'How will you be paying for that?'
'No man is ever going to understand me like Richard Linklater did.'
'Paper or plastic?'
'Nobody is ever going to understand me like Richard Linklater did.'

Ignoring the fact that Richard Linklater, while liking me fine and thinking I was a good writer, did not actually know me well enough to attempt to understand me, let alone be the only man who had ever got it right.

It is terrible to be almost there and have it taken away, so much harder than the times I've not stood a chance, and it's a humbling echo of the romantic experience. The love-bombing before they turn on you.

My cable television got cut off and then my mobile. And when several of my agent's other girl writers bought homes in the Hollywood Hills, I realised it had to happen.

Never, ever mention anyone else during any break-up. It has to be about you and the person you're leaving, not you and wild suspicions about others. But I couldn't help myself.

'How is, uh, Girl Writer X doing?'

He told me about her various films, but added:

'Look, she would rather be earning $600,000 a year and making art like you.'

'I'm *not* making $600k a year. I'm about to lose my health insurance.'

We stayed on the phone for an hour and a half. I could hear the cars and knew he was outside the office, smoking the cigarettes he had just given up. That is *so* him, I thought fondly.

I struggled with it over many nights. But I couldn't stop thinking about the other women.

At the behest of the director with whom my agent had brokered a peace, I moved to *his* agency.

Oh, I know full well that things fall apart: movie deals, relationships, love. All of this is transient. You can't put a pin through love. But you *can* with film. That's why I wanted so much to make it. And then other people can reach out to the screen and feel those characters as if they had, as Billy Wilder said of Monroe, touched warm flesh.

I didn't want power from my work. I just wanted them to know that I'd been here, a hairpin down the headboard. And when you get to make your own movie, write the script and direct it too, you are not only the one who dropped it, but the hairpin and the headboard, too.

The great man I moved to LA for turned out not to be so great.

But the fact remains: he is the reason I moved to LA and in ten years it gave me motherhood, my debut film, a big house on the water, a view from the top. And it gave me divorce, too. It gave me the plane ride back to London. So when, having returned to the city you grew up in – the place that first shamed you, with cold days and dark by 4 p.m. – you start to tremble at these memories, hold tight your two hot-water bottles and weighted sensory penguin. You're OK. You're going to be OK. In the end.

When that mother had looked at my top-floor flat and asked, 'How did this happen to you?', I didn't know her well enough to explain it in the simplest terms. I ended up here as a knock-on result of my self-esteem problem: it was too high and disaster followed.

I didn't know her well enough to tell her that, when I got my body at fourteen, but before anyone had seen it, I was so amazed by the sight in the full-length mirror, I imagined men crying tears of joy in gratitude at being allowed to see me naked. That isn't what happened. They said things, but not that, and *I* spent from sixteen to twenty-six feeling a debt of gratitude to men who wanted me. That's why it takes young women a while to figure out what they're into sexually. Because they're so absorbed in feeling grateful for being wanted.

The first night Ben stayed over, it was ostensibly to watch *The Night of the Iguana*. We started kissing on the sofa under the gaze of Richard Burton. Then we moved into the bedroom, where he made it onto the mattress first and I undressed in the doorway you're meant to stand under if there is an earthquake.

'Oh my God!' Ben gasped and began to cry.

Dropping my underwear to the floor with my denim skirt, I looked up, alarmed.

'What is it?'

'You're just so beautiful.'

So I very quickly married him. The fourteen-year-old me had preprogrammed this to happen.

As soon as Ben stepped out of his clothes on that first night, my cats stepped into them, as if bagsying him for themselves and for me.

I'd sold two pilots that season and my apartment rental was very grand – I'd selected it to withstand earthquakes and for glamour (in LA, the two can be combined and often are). To live inside one is to strive for the same qualities.

The terrible thing about West Hollywood that year was that although I was used to seeing the long-term homeless, we began to see many people newly homeless, their suitcases of belongings with them, the look of utter confusion on their faces as they stepped between worlds. I thought of heartbreak, when the relationship is first over and you are suddenly out there alone. Ben befriended one young homeless man who had a dog. The young man would often buzz our flat and Ben would give him cash and buy him dog food. There came a point when Ben was away filming and I, answering the doorbell alone, pregnant, had to acknowledge to myself I was touched by the boy and his dog, but also scared of them, and *that* felt like love, too.

When we first got together, Ben lived in a guest house at the very top of Laurel Canyon, with a view that felt like the end of the world and cupboards that seemed prepared for it. I'd wake to find him missing from the bed, having left me love letters on Final Reminder bills.

He'd be gone, having got up to smoke and, unable to get back to sleep, driven his truck to the 24-hour Duane Reade in the Valley – the 'Britney Spears' pharmacy where she'd wander the aisles during her breakdown. Sometimes I'd wake up to the smell of his cigarettes and piles and piles of stationery supplies and know he was back.

What is there to be gained from retracing the past like this, walking your backstreets because your own buses are on diversion?

'When did the olden days become the now days?' my daughter recently asked and it seemed to me like asking where your arse ends and your upper thigh begins. Perhaps that's why it's an area of such focus in workouts. If you could differentiate *that*, there might be much more you could clarify in your life.

On some of the Final Demand envelopes up in that guest house, Ben had just written my name over and over. One becomes resentful of the person who makes you feel so overwhelmed. I eventually became a bill to pay, a chore, the worst thing you can be. And then at the end, the person whose name you've written over and over on the envelope is, inevitably, a disconnect notice.

But before I could think of the best answer for our daughter, she had a new query:

'Is the lady who sang "The White Cliffs of Dover" the same lady who sang "Kids in America"?'

We got married in the two-bedroom penthouse of the Chateau Marmont, my favourite Los Angeles hotel.

There was a harbinger, at the wedding, our union might present challenges. One being the hora a friend initiated on the penthouse balcony. Balancing on top of our chairs, our eyes locked as the tipsy guests pumped us up and down on their shoulders, the moon above us and the traffic of Sunset Strip far below, we were both terrified we would die being tipped over the shallow edge. Besides our own tumultuous personal histories, the Jews could not have survived so much, over so many centuries, only for Ben and I to meet our end in such a stupid way.

Another harbinger: the night before, for my hen do, my favourite women had rented a suite in the same hotel. We wore pyjamas, got pizzas and beers and each brought our most-watched film from our teen years. We stayed up half the night watching *Dirty Dancing* and *The Craft*.

In the morning, my friends Elishia and Andrea, stretching awake on sofas, asked if there was anything they could do for me before the wedding. I said, sure, they could fetch the flowers from the market. They thought I meant go and collect bunches of colourful blooms that had been ordered in my name. What I really meant was just go and pick out some flowers, I don't care what you get or in which shade. My friends came through beautifully, arranging all the individual blooms themselves in their own designs before changing, dirt-smudged and sweaty, in the toilets minutes before the ceremony. They still laugh about how I didn't know flower arrangements are an integral decision when planning a wedding. Maybe if I'd known to care about the flower arrangements, I wouldn't be divorced . . . Maybe.

In getting hitched, we had agreed to travel together, always. The promise was infinite – like the horizon seen from Highway 1. Seven days by car on a road famous for its hairpin bends seemed a real way to dip our toes in that unquantifiable 'forever'. Travelling across California all the way from San Francisco back home to LA, there were fancy beds, treetop bunks, yurts and sleeping bags. We could be happy with each other anywhere and so high/low living had always been our way. We could also be *unhappy* anywhere . . . When we fought, it was like having a cold and not being able to imagine I would ever again not have one, even though I knew logically it would one day pass.

We began in Sausalito at The Inn Above Tide, a boutique hotel in a picture-postcard town across the bridge from San Francisco, where all twenty-nine rooms face the bay. When we checked in, we were still getting our breath back from the wedding. So many people had flown in from Australia and London, the customs man at LAX said to one Melbourne-ite, 'You must be here for Ben and Emma's wedding.'

After the pressure of the wedding week, maybe it's no surprise that the first night of our honeymoon was explosive in the wrong way. A disagreement followed us up the corridor like the camera in *The West Wing*. By the time we got to dinner, it was an argument so toxic that I grabbed a bread knife and stormed out into the street. (I didn't know what to do with the knife except maybe butter a loaf, but that's kind of a bullshit take from a girl who had just written a whole book about suicide.) I curled up in a ball in a doorway. I knew I was being ridiculous and obscene. As a wedding party favour, we'd handed out pre-printed argument-solving cards that said: 'I am being a dick but I don't know how to stop.' Unfortunately, there were none in my pocket.

He followed, yelling. The waiters smiled benignly. There should be a TripAdvisor site for restaurants in which to argue. Poggio Trattoria scored highly.

When dawn broke, we woke to a view that was just so lovely and instead of turning the car around, we turned the fight around. From our teak private deck, we watched the play of light on San Francisco Bay. Water is a good thing when you're feeling stuck, because it's always moving, even imperceptibly. A room with a view (with a sunken bath) gave us back our perspective. I will always credit The Inn Above Tide with saving our marriage. The first night of it, anyway. There would be many other nights in our lives to be saved – in the life of any committed couple – and views would always come in handy. Bunkers can protect you from bombs, but it is hard to cope with an *emotional* shock in a basement flat.

Thus tested, it felt right that we should be heading to Big Sur, the nadir of Elizabeth Taylor and Richard Burton's tumultuous love affair, where they filmed *The Sandpiper*, in which she played a bohemian artist and he the priest she seduces. Mining a different screen romance, we stayed at Deetjens, a rustic cabin compound deep in The Redwoods, where I imagined he was a cowboy and I was a saloon girl (I was thinking Robert Mitchum and Marilyn Monroe in *River of No Return*).

Now we'd made up, the sight of my husband's ringed finger on my waist thrilled me and we spent probably our most romantic night there. The fact that there was no TV, internet or mobile reception made it easier to lose ourselves. We listened to Joni Mitchell under the wooden beams and dusky lamplight. The giant trees blocked out the real world and we only crawled out of our quaint floral bed for Deetjens' pancake breakfast.

One of the most famous landmarks in Big Sur is the new age 'self-actualisation' retreat, Esalen Institute (parodied in the Natalie Wood film *Bob & Carol & Ted & Alice*). It has a fabled communal hot tub built into a cliff face jutting out over the Pacific Ocean. But Ben refused to visit Esalen: 'I don't want to go to the wife-swapping institute on our first week of marriage!'

We headed, instead, to the Big Sur Bakery, where the amount of attention Ben felt he was getting cemented his notion that Big Sur is a swingers' haven.

'They want to sex us even more now we're married!'

With sex on the brain, we visited The Henry Miller Library, a kind of cultural general store. We bought several of his novels, along with Ella Fitzgerald and Duke

Ellington vinyl. It's the only place in Big Sur with mobile reception – which we tried not to let break our spell as we headed to our next spot.

Treebones Resort was our cheapest stop along Highway 1. A campsite on an ocean cliff, where we spent the night huddling close in subservient awe of nature. You can stay in a pre-built yurt (a kind of luxury teepee), bring your own tent or brave the 'Human Nest' – a man-made bird's nest up a tree overlooking the waves. But we were determined to construct our own shelter and that we managed it without recrimination against each other or the tent felt like a significant achievement for two hot-headed people. We rewarded ourselves with spicy tuna rolls and saki at the resort's darkly lit sushi bar (luxury sushi at a cheapo campsite felt strange and very sexy – two things successfully existing in opposition is a concept I wish I had remembered better as things fell apart).

The Post Ranch Inn has to be placed at the end of any trip down Highway 1, because it really can't be topped. It is outrageously luxurious but, like love, it's all in the details: the free-standing cabins either built into the cliff faces or attached to the trees; the cashmere bedding; the massages with views of the mountains; complimentary yoga in a yurt; two basking pools; the minibar of your dreams – the best pecans, the best truffles, the artisan chocolate-chip cookies, the fresh milk. Then there's all the Post Ranch Inn's hidden spots – handmade wooden benches, hammocks off the trail path – where even young couples in love get to lose themselves alone (something I suspect keeps a marriage alive wherever you are).

I noted that their welcome pack advises how to react if you see a mountain lion:

> Mountain lions want to avoid confrontation. Do not run – it may stimulate lion's instinct to chase. Do all you can to appear larger than you are – raise your arms and open your jacket.

I didn't want confrontation either and decided to utilise the advice in marital fights. How quickly I forgot to appear bigger than I am.

'I want to bring my parents here,' I said.

'We will,' he promised. 'I'm going to get very rich.'

His vision board fantasies annoyed me – I didn't think they were reasonable. Why does he want to make many millions a year? Why can't he want to make a million a year? I laugh darkly many years later when he tells me he *is* making many millions that year, when it is not mine to share.

How do you follow impeccable elegance and luxury? John Waters-style trash! Getting inland, we arrived at Madonna Inn, a motel in San Luis Obispo created by a Vegas showgirl who found Christ. Each room is themed – the Caveman Room built out of rock or Love Birds an attic room done out in reds and pinks with gilded mirrors, perfect for nesting with your new lover, Liberace. After all the views, fresh air and expansive horizon, we loved our night shut indoors watching terrible reality TV and eating pasta with pink sauce followed by pink cake with pink frosting. Our hearts were bursting with contentment and acid reflux.

California is just so vast, like a marriage – you don't ever have to leave it, because there's everything possible if you're willing to live low and live high, and never stop exploring.

When things were hopeless, I tried to call on memories of pink frosting, wide blue skies, darkened chintzy rooms and redwoods cradling us. To cherish the fact that two such hurt people had found each other, to feel awe about that. But California also hinges on a fault line and I kept on feeling shocks.

After our wedding, we moved to a place in Studio City, which we rented for the garden and the floor-to-ceiling living-room windows that flooded the place with light. According to the art of Ed Ruscha, Studio City is quintessential Los Angeles. In that house, I felt myself get pregnant in two parts. First, through the intercourse itself – how my body dragged him in, like the feeling of sand around your feet when the tides are strong (soon enough, a major fight and he was gone). And secondly, in a hotel to get away from the empty marital home, I remember feeling a jolt of electricity moving down my body as I lay in bed watching movies on demand, eating room service. That was me, becoming pregnant, as the home test (or rather, hotel room test) quickly confirmed. I carefully wrapped up the test and then, as if controlled by the forces in *The Manchurian Candidate*, put my two-decade vegetarianism aside to pick up the phone and order a steak, rare.

The night we decided to make a go of it, we watched a crack begin to run down the wall of the room where we had conceived. A structural engineer came to check the foundations, said our house could collapse any minute, red-flagged it, and we moved out the next day. As soon as we did, we realised our dream house had been set at an angle that, despite being in LA, was very dark. The floor-to-ceiling windows that had so impressed us weren't flooding the room with light at all – they were letting in *darkness*. What hope was there for us if we could not see the difference between darkness and light? As artists, we function at the intersection of those places, but, in maintaining a domestic life, it is problematic.

CJ was born and was a lucky baby, because Ben's employment and earnings soared. Soon, we owned our moderne with an 'e' house. Overwhelmed, perhaps, at what was in our reach, we never did anything to make the garden look pretty. On the contrary, sometimes Ben found sidewalk furniture that had been discarded – an armchair with a sobbing clown painted into the pillows – and he put it in the centre of our garden to get rained on. But it was ours.

And as messy as the interior often was, the view beyond the ship-in-motion windows was always transcendent. The birds skimming the water before taking flight, in transfixing formations, at sunset. With nightfall, the lights reflecting on the reservoir from all the little houses carved into the surrounding hills. Why would you want to look inwards to fix things, when looking out brings instant relief?

Owned and maintained by the Los Angeles Department of Water and Power, the reservoir is the focal point of the community. It comprises two concrete-bottomed basins. If you walked down there, you'd see the reservoir is surrounded by a running trail, a picnic lawn, a basketball court, a kids' playground and a dog park. A loop trail goes round the water for two and a half miles, so you only have to do the circuit once to get a good workout and it's the right length so conversation with a walking partner gets to build but never lull. The loop sits, in the Californian section of my brain, alongside Kandinsky's circle paintings hanging at the Norton Simon Museum in Pasadena.

I befriended strangers and remained pen pals with them as they taught their toddlers to walk along the chain-link fence that stops anyone from entering the water. But I don't need to get that close. I only need the view, that play of light on water that, despite its concrete basin, is always incrementally moving. It is a *reservoir*: it is beautiful, and it is back-up. At times of forest fire, helicopters hover over it, sucking up water. No matter how hard things have become at home, I live in the shadow of safety and so a part of me that's both California-mystical and British-ly responsive to prominent signposting feels safe.

The overnight draining of all the water in the reservoirs was a neighbourhood talking point – except the neighbours seemed less energised to talk once it happened. There were bleak rumours that the water had become contaminated with the cancer-causing chemical bromate. Or that the water was being repurposed for a part of LA that needed it more.

For two whole years, they became moon craters outside our ship-in-motion windows – now, our house was a ship on dry land. Without the water, irritations such as biting insects and creepy spiders were gone, but so was the 'snap out of it' magic. It messed up my belief that I'd be OK, the loss of that reservoir. In my capacity as part of the collective unconscious, I *was* the water. I was the beautiful view I was looking at (which wasn't a beautiful view any more).

People stopped talking about it after a while because it was too depressing or too divisive (between houses that were by the reservoirs versus houses that looked down on them).

That this fundamental change in scenery threw some of us so badly was not because we couldn't accept change. It was because a change was coming, a change that you haven't asked for, and that you must now prepare for. Not like the change of leaves, because that's natural. And that's British (LA has no visible seasons). This was an unnatural occurrence to a man-made object.

I always liked that I could be looking at the reservoir but thinking of the ocean an hour away in Malibu – that LA waters were dripping through my daydreams and into each other. I'd wanted the house because I'd fallen in love with the water. Ben made my wish come true. And the LA Department of Water and Power took it away. The California dream had so flatteringly lit our view of each other when we first met. What malignant force might taint it next?

Part Three

＊

If you carry anxiety about reaching your forties at the moment your husband achieves wealth, acclaim and celebrity, try adding the ascent of Donald Trump. The soon-to-be president's oft-proclaimed horror of middle-aged women is one voice in your head, the messages to your husband's Facebook from far-flung young women is another. They are, in the bikini shots and nudes they DM your husband, beautiful (vulgar but beautiful), while Trump is the epitome of physical ugliness. Not like someone with a disease or a victim of a chimp attack, who might still have a bright light inside them, but someone whose standard human face has been corroded by his hideous personality and psychological mis-wiring. It's a face that is frightening to behold and it is also omnipresent.

Maybe, somewhere deep down, it's what seeded the concept of draining my sexuality. We weren't having sex anyway. Having to look at Donald Trump did not make me want to fuck.

There was also a knock-on effect that came from watching two people, who don't want to make love or even touch or stand near each other, lead the world. The Donald–Melania relationship was *so* dysfunctional, it may have poisoned other couples who might otherwise have made it.

Trump's presidency ran in parallel with my feelings for my ex-husband, whom I divorced a month after the election and whom I have long considered a stand-in for Trump. Both men are endlessly affronted, ill-tempered, ostentatious, wounded in childhood, dominant and deeply eccentric. It's just that Ben is also sweet and handsome, funny, clever and enormously talented.

And, unlike Trump, my ex-husband has windows of understanding how differently he is wired compared to the people around him. Trump is the disruptive vote, just like Ben. In early baby photos of CJ, he lovingly cradles her while smoking, sweating and wearing an Angelyne 'the Billboard Queen' T-shirt. In the days after we filed for divorce, while still sharing the same home, on my floor I play 'I see A Darkness' by Johnny Cash and on his floor he blasts 'Born to be Alive', the tinny minor disco classic by Patrick Hernandez. A disruptor of my grieving process.

By the time Trump was elected and I filed for divorce, I had drained that part of me. I didn't just give up sex – I gave up tampons and switched to period pants that are not only exterior, but also *disgusting* – a Sheela-na-gig-level horror show. For almost five years after the election of Donald J. Trump, as every fibre screamed 'Get him the hell away from this country I so love,' nothing and nobody was allowed inside – not even me – so vigilant did the Trump term make me.

The world's most terrible man was also the world's most powerful man and my instinct was to keep every single one of them away, just in case.

And so I decided to make what was happening organically anyway into something concrete: I took a vow of celibacy for the term of Trump's presidency. It seemed like a good idea for someone whose life had been guided, thus far, by romantic obsession.

And though it may sound psychotic, it actually helped. It helped me to come back to my real size. I became *so* my real size that there was no space for anyone at all to enter. But did that mean I'd gone full circle – walked the perimeter of the reservoir – and made myself tiny?

'You've stopped flirting completely. You've turned everything off,' said Jemima Kirke, who had starred with her sister Lola in the film I'd written and directed right before my divorce.

She had, herself, just got divorced and, in the process, begun dating a young musician who left her a trail of rare books hidden across the city for her to find when he had to leave on tour.

I'm not saying it's because they drained 'my' reservoir, but the main thing I allowed inside me apart from songs through headphones was glass after glass of water. It affronted me that, beyond every other despicable thing about him, Trump – a rich person with access to the best food and lifestyle! – was proudly unhealthy. In my fantasies of his death, it was ultimately his poor diet that did him in.

Water and the absence of it kept cropping up, still, when I moved to London. A mother from school asked me to join her for a swim in her apartment pool – these were everywhere in LA, where kids held pool parties for their birthdays that fully kitted-out 'mermaids' would host, but pools are a true rarity in North London. I found a polite way to get out of it because I didn't want my body being viewed, not even benignly. Even in London, I felt Trump's/Ben's gaze.

I didn't think I was unattractive because Trump hates middle-aged women or because Ben had a young girl-friend. I didn't think I wasn't still a prospect. There's nothing I found very wrong with my body, it's just that it was completely and totally private. That's why I was safe. The notion of existing as a sexual being was gone from my memory, a password I'd carefully saved somewhere I couldn't remember.

A constant in the news was the awfulness of young girls having their lives fall apart through stolen clips transmitted across the internet. This sexuality, for these four years, is mine mine mine! You can't have it. You can't look at it. It's through my own lens held up to the light projection of my own memories. I curse those terrible things happening to girls by phones and in their phones.

Giving up sex was a way of walking out of the movie even if you have to push past knees and handbags to do so. It was saying – at the age a woman is considered to be of decreasing sexual currency, so they must twist themselves in knots emotionally and physically to continue getting chosen for the team – 'I'm not playing this game.' It was enough, through an apocalyptic presidential term, to ask nothing of my body other than it work.

Celibacy was not only bearable, it was *epic* – a place inside myself where a woman can run late at night with headphones in her ears and not have to feel afraid.

Why doesn't he/she love me? is the place every girl and woman and man comes to again and again while processing heartbreak. When that's not the real question – the real question is Why do I love him or her? The former cannot be answered and is therefore a form of procrastination and surrender to perseveration. But the second – Why do I love him or her? – is answerable, though it takes hard work.

If you examine what exactly it is that it's fulfilling, you may find there are other places from which you can get those feelings. It's an inventory that takes focus and will give you focus, whereas the first is diffuse. It's saying 'It's in God's hands,' because you're not ready or brave enough to have it in your hands. It's OK not to be brave enough, but you have to know that's what's going on so you can work towards being ready in your own time. You have to know *when* to put things in God's hands and when in yours. It's like the combo of psych meds and talk therapy.

I made the decision that celibacy was the right place to figure all of this out. It was an arbitrary decision, but they can be the best. I learned that from directing: there are times you're going to have to make quick decisions, knowing that they may be the wrong ones.

Donald Trump being president – the anxiety and the fear and the looking at his repulsive face – didn't make me want to have sex and I decided I'd just wait it out until he was gone. As a teen, I couldn't wait one whole day for my mother to wonder if I'd developed anorexia before I gave up and switched to the instant gratification of cutting. But *this* I would have patience with. Because not everything you put conscious effort into has to be an act of self-harm. Pregnancy and novel-writing aside, this may be the first time that concept really hit me.

It was a bigger, more exciting challenge because I had just turned forty and felt very squarely in my sexual prime. If you live your sexual prime alone, that energy doesn't just vanish. It alchemises. The energy went everywhere – the almost five years I abstained from sex were, without question, the most fertile years of my life.

But Trump wouldn't always be there. I wouldn't always be licking my wounds from a freshly failed marriage. I knew it might be good to remember where I put this particular password one day.

I have a secret. I'm not proud of it, nor am I ashamed.

When I am particularly stressed about work, I buy a jumbo bag of sweets, take a bin, then chew and spit out each piece, methodically, until the entire bag is gone. Unconnected to weight maintenance, it isn't bulimia per se, as none of it can be brought up since none of it ever gets swallowed.

Ben once walked in on me as I was coolly spitting a miniature Snickers into the bin. Before he could say anything, I blurted 'I chew and spit sweets when I'm worried.'

He kissed the top of my head and said, 'You do you. Funny little Fozzy,' and then he went back to his video game, which he'd been playing for seven hours.

It's complicated for damaged people to try to create their own version of family. Perhaps it would have been healthier if we'd been less understanding of each other's quirks.

Ben would also sometimes walk in on me writing as I was sniffing a pair of my worn panties. I've always been comforted by the smell of my own underwear, which has the same narcotic effect on me as the stuffed toy I've cherished since infanthood. Ben would smile, say, 'Funny little Fozzy,' and walk out again. He understood: if you covet your own used panties, what kind of a deviant does that make you? A very gentle one.

I do get this nagging pang, from inside this lockdown – how much I turned myself on, and always had. You could ask if I've ever explored what it's about, but I already know: as with several of my heightened emotional states, it's about a Tom Petty video.

When I talk about abstaining from sex as part of the post-divorce process of 'coming back to my real size', a vital memory, at a pivotal age, was the Tom Petty and the Heartbreakers clip for 'Don't Come Round Here No More'. When I was a kid, around eleven, I had a room at the top of our house and a small TV in my bedroom. I used to fall asleep each night listening to *Rumours* by Fleetwood Mac. West Coast pop was under my pre-adolescent skin, marking me for a Californian marriage twenty years later. My favourite was 'The Chain', on side B. I loved how, right when you had melted into it, the tempo changed – long into adulthood, I would recognise it as a simulacrum of great sex.

But my favourite video was the Heartbreaker's reinterpretation of *Alice in Wonderland*, Petty as the Mad Hatter leering at a teenage Alice. I adore Tom Petty but have no sexual thoughts about him except that video is the core beating heart of my sexual being. The song itself: the disconcerting chord changes, the lack of care or concern for his love interest. Her courage, her oppression, the gaslighting, her little round mouth. 'I don't feel you any more.' We sexualise the thing that is most distressing to us to make it safe. It's why women sometimes ask to be called a whore in bed.

I knew 'I don't feel you any more' was absolutely devastating, and I was just a kid.

For forty years, from new wave hero to alt-country troubadour, Petty had a face that says 'Yes, I am a strange-looking blond man, but my lyrics are *transcendent*.'

'I don't feel you any more.' Because they once felt you. The man. The city once felt you alive and valid and desirable, and you laughed as you walked because you knew they were right.

Tom Petty and the Heartbreakers gather around Alice as it becomes apparent to her that she is the cake at the centre of the tea party. And it ends like this: the men slice her up and make her eat herself. It was the first time I came.

But if there was to be no more sex until Trump was out of office, if that was the decision I had come to, then there were clothes that should be put away. Clothes for drawing men to me and clothes heavy with sexual memory. Do like the Italians and put them away for the season. Make space for something, even if you don't know what it is.

Some of my clothes are so dense with longing they felt harder to fold than they ought to be, pushing back against my fingers as the memory expands:

The Marilyn Monroe Dress

A pale blue cotton wiggle dress with white Swiss dot embroidery. I was looking for a dress to replicate one I saw in a photograph of a sleeping Marilyn Monroe by Eve Arnold. From a decade when there were separate departments for 'day' dresses and 'evening' dresses, this is not an item of clothing you're ever meant to actually find – it should be a quest, a riddle that can't be solved, your Rosebud.

But in 1994, the now defunct New York fashion brand Tocca included something spookily similar in their very first collection – and proceeded to bring one out each season. I can still see the arched brow of the saleswoman (at my youth and my carefully counted bills). I wonder if finding that dress was a *Sliding Doors* wormhole to a thrilling but perilous love life. That I paid cash seems to have exacerbated its power.

The dress never fails, even twenty-five years after I bought it. But it's like Mickey and the broomsticks in *Fantasia*. I wore it at nineteen and kept it on as I seduced an older man I was crazy about – a man who was palpably scared of me until we had sex, then he could tell I didn't know what I was doing. I was wearing it at thirty-two, in the first paparazzi photo with a movie star after we'd eluded their notice for so many months. Then twenty-two years after I bought it, it was stuck to my post-baby body in the humid summer air of a location shoot.

My husband's co-star, who had been barbecuing for the cast, checked no one else was in the room, then murmured 'Mama. Try this.' His fingers touched my lips as he fed me. Nothing else happened between us. But the memory of his fingers on my lips kept me going a long time.

Marc Jacobs Jumper with Childish Hearts

I wore it to the abortion I was having because I felt I was too young to have a baby. Something compelled me to dress in my own defence: I am too young! I loved my boyfriend madly, but we had recently broken up and he'd gone home to New Zealand. I was twenty-five and he had a 45-year-old baby mama who he was no longer with but could not separate from. I was the younger woman in that equation.

Well-intentioned friends told him it would pain her too greatly to have to meet me because of my extreme youth. In fact, it was the oldest I had ever been. I thought of it when, in my forties, I met my ex-husband's 25-year-old girlfriend – I think the second girlfriend he'd had after our break-up. He was away but said I could crash at the LA house. She and I smoked weed together and then she retired to my marital bed, while I went down to the guest room and slept the sleep of the just. I was relieved not to be married to him any more. I loved him dearly, but he was hectic and I was forty-one and just wanted life beyond *Thunderdome*.

But at twenty-five, I was addicted to hectic.

I should not have fallen into the arms of my ex-boyfriend when he rang my doorbell unannounced a week after the abortion. When he went back to New Zealand, I gave him one of my earrings – worse, they were my baby bangles that Mum had converted into hoop earrings as an eighteenth birthday gift.

I was never sorry I had the abortion. I think of my ex very rarely and when I do, I remember him as controlling and selfish. I would be shocked if he had any fond memories of me. When I think about my mother, who is eighty-three, being gone one day, I am incapacitated with a grief I know is barely even a dress rehearsal. I am fearful, when she does pass, that I may go on a transcontinental quest to recover the missing hoop earring.

The Band T-Shirt

In photos, I was very slim and there are only stolen glimpses of this Bruce Springsteen & The E Street Band T-shirt, which seems appropriate since the man who gave it to me was someone I was having an affair with. He lived in a Californian mansion and I lived in a tiny New York studio where the landlord couldn't believe my parents didn't have enough money to co-sign.

The first time he took me to his bedroom, he opened this bottom drawer and it was entirely full of vintage rock T-shirts. All these rock T-shirts could be yours! I had seen this gesture in Douglas Sirk's *Written on the Wind*, where Lauren Bacall's would-be paramour shows her a drawer of glass-beaded purses to choose from.

I did a really shitty thing, which was wear it to keep the feeling of him near even when I was with my boyfriend. As I've said, I was very in love with my boyfriend, but he had not or could not cede control from the mother of his child. On numerous occasions over a year and a half, I was made to wait in cars because she would not let me meet her kid. They sensed something toxic in me. I guess I thought they might not be wrong. I guess I figured if they considered me toxic, I'd be toxic.

Which led me to this affair. To have the man you love, but who won't commit to you, have his hands on your breasts under the T-shirt given to you by the man who is available and pursuing you . . . It was an elixir for a 25-year-old testing their emotional volume control. Springsteen may famously be a family man, but the T-shirt was tissue thin – it had had other lives. Maybe its original owner did worse things than me.

The secret lover was many decades older than me and as manipulative as a teenager. I had a big bottom back then and he'd say it was difficult to feel attracted to his ex-wife because she had no arse. But he was also sweet. He'd ask to talk to my mother on the phone. He'd invite my parents to his mansion. You can be manipulative and tender at the same time, which was the essence of where I also found myself in my mid-twenties.

The Springsteen T-shirt is one of the few items that hasn't survived my move back to London. I don't know what happened to it. It is gone, worn thinner into the ether, dust to dust. It's just gone. I have felt a great liberation since I got divorced, apart from when I come across a photo of myself in this T-shirt.

I took an erotic pleasure in the marital moral code for the seven years I was with my husband. But now it's over, I see this T-shirt and get overwhelmed with a sorrow that at first I couldn't place. Eventually, I realised what I was mourning: I may never get to be dishonest again. The man who gave it to me *wasn't* my great love, but I miss our furtiveness. Our secret language.

It hurts me, shames me even, that I don't have anything in my life I could call a secret. That I am at the age where everything *is* as it appears to be: that I look tired because I am tired. That I gained weight because I eat more than when I was thin. That thin isn't everything or anything, but at least it was a system of my own, by me, for me. Like an affair.

The Fuck-You Outfit

I had not heard from my husband in almost a year – he'd almost completely dropped from contact – when he called on 23 December to ask me to be in San Francisco the next day with our daughter, where he was working, so we could have Christmas together. He shouted, then he called back and begged and pleaded, and the only way I could make myself go was if I went dressed as Joan Crawford.

This was how I would express my blazing anger at him. A skin-tight ink-black long-sleeved top with hooks and eyes from top to bottom. A black pencil skirt. Bettie Page fetish heels from Prada. Stockings. A corset. I was so uncomfortable. But I wanted to look and feel like a superstructure, a piece of architecture, something that would be standing upright long, long after he was gone.

If he noticed he didn't say. Just like when I waited for him to acknowledge how tiny our temporary London flat was, instead he walked in and said, 'Wow! You guys landed on your feet!' He did, however, call and ask if he could give my number to a friend of his who had been rhapsodic about my outfit. I politely declined and he said, 'Well, if you change your mind . . .'

The Fifties Dream Girl

A knee-length cream tea dress by Maison Mayle, which had ruffled sleeves, a bow around the waist and delicate orange-pink Hawaiian print. It was incredibly feminine.

My ex-husband ultimately says that how I was dressed was a miscue, that he'd gone out that night very much hoping to meet the woman he would marry and I was dressed like a fifties housewife, alluring but compliant. And that he married me and found I wasn't like that at all.

The Power Dresser

Red velvet Alice McCall skirt with giant ochre flowers and black Brandon Maxwell scuba fabric top. All of the lawyers gathered to hammer out the terms of divorce could see what he'd lost, but he couldn't because he was wearing pitch-black glasses indoors. When I handed him a Vegemite sandwich wrapped in foil that I'd prepared in anticipation of the terrible mood he falls into when hungry, that did not go well. All that I had gained in the lawyers' eyes through my strong, independent dress sense was lost at the sight of my needy salty sandwich.

A Dress to Meet the Girlfriend In

We were at least a year from the divorce coming through and he was head over heels in love with a girl from enormous wealth, though he hadn't told me about her yet. My daughter and I met him and a few of his fellow actors in Paris for a hotel tea. My kid had on a raincoat and wellington boots, and I had a pink plaid A-line Vampire's Wife skirt with glass buttons down the front. Gucci over-knee nylons with black velvet bows up the back. His young love was dressed like a teenage boy and terribly hungover.

Though I didn't know they were together, some sixth sense was looking out for me, because she might have been an astonishing beauty, but I pulled it together that day. She slumped in her chair, denim dungarees crumpling, eyeliner dripping, her extraordinary face a mask of exhaustion. I held myself with dignity because my clothes were holding me upright.

As the chemistry between them began to dawn on me, I asked if I could try on her leather jacket and she handed it over gingerly while he looked at the ground. While waiting outside for a taxi, an older man approached me and tried to pick me up. I remember how shocked I was the first few times that happened when I moved to New York at twenty-one: a stranger approaching me, in a comic book shop, or when I was sheltering from the rain outside a department store, or coming out of a bar to catch up with me after they noticed me walking up the street. It happened either because I was a once-in-a-generation beauty (doubtful), because New Yorkers, despite what you've heard, are very friendly (possible), or because I was extremely young (likely). But that time in Paris, my kid still in the lobby with my ex and his new love, was the last time a complete stranger has ever hit on me, apart from . . .

Clothes to Run Away In

I was taking my daughter to the South Bank. We'd often get through a Saturday by riding a bus to the Tube to the Thames clipper boat. A few stops from Embankment Underground Station, a blind man engaged me in conversation and then asked for my help getting off the train. I wished he'd asked someone who was not a woman on their own, wrangling a very small child, but he asked me. And she was at the age when helping a stranger in need is as exciting as taking drugs.

After I'd guided him to the platform, he leaned in and whispered in my ear 'Don't worry, I'm not going to rape you both.'

I took my little girl's hand and ran through the station to the exit. I thought my Marni boots, with their block heels, were chic but sensible, but as I was running, they didn't feel sensible at all. She couldn't understand why I'd dumped a blind man and raged at me for hours. She wouldn't talk to me or walk with me. I rang her dad, went to another room to explain what had happened and asked if he could get through to her in a way that wouldn't be scary.

He told her 'The man said the rudest thing you can say.'

She calmed down. My feet were blistered. But it was the first time post-divorce I felt like we were co-parenting.

The Plain White T-Shirt

The day we moved to London from LA, before we left, my daughter's father came by to hug her but couldn't face being the one to drive us to the airport. Scott, the kind producer on my film who had become my loyal friend, offered to give us a lift. Scott had once stood guard outside the editing-room door when two of the other male producers were trying to wrestle the cut from me. Now, he loaded our bags into the boot of his Land Rover.

I was wearing a plain white V-neck T-shirt that I'd bought on a trip my husband and I made to Santa Fe, New Mexico when we first got together. Our hostess then was Porochista Khakpour, an Iranian–American academic of great beauty and charm. Ben was appalled that her boyfriend swam naked in the hot tub and didn't help her to carry the groceries in from the car. She was with me when I bought the T-shirt in a local yoga studio after we did a vigorous class. It was whisper thin, flatteringly cut and worn so much it ultimately got tiny holes. I traced the company to Vancouver and they sent another T-shirt. By the time I wore that one through, their phone was disconnected and they weren't traceable any more. In the span of my marriage and white V-neck T-shirts, Porochista got crippling Lyme disease.

The white V-neck tee conjures, immediately, Marlon Brando, a wistful yearning for Americana in which to leave the country. This was compounded by the fact that I also had on a Disneyland hat with my name sewn between the Mickey ears. When I left, and for a year after, Ben and I were in a very bad period. When we were in the same room, he would not talk to me or acknowledge me. In our final days in LA, he'd taken our daughter to Disneyland and I had said, 'Buy me a Minnie Mouse hat with my name embroidered on it' and I wasn't sure he'd even heard, since he would not look at me. But he did, still not meeting my eye when he handed it over. It was a kind of test I'd invented. I don't know what I was testing.

The white T-shirt was a clean slate and a window to the past, a window back to the start. When we didn't know each other, just fancied each other like crazy. Now we knew each other inside out, Porochista was confined to a wheelchair and the T-shirt has been washed so many times it is translucent.

Work Gear

When I directed my first movie, I wanted to distract my cast and crew visually from the possibility that I didn't know what the fuck I was doing. I had seen photographs of Sofia Coppola in a utilitarian khaki jumpsuit she'd had specially made by Sonia Rykiel and wore every day to direct *The Beguiled*. That was her sixth film. This was my first and I went way the other way, in dresses stamped with cactus print, a tartan blue-and-red swing skirt, green platform heels, a bright pink dress covered with Frida Kahlo and the Virgin Mary. I had on the latter the day I had to shoot my not yet but soon-to-be ex-husband passionately kissing Lola Kirke.

Ben said, 'Just fucking show me how you want me to kiss her,' so I did, pulling him to me.

My cinematographer later confessed she'd been rolling when he and I embraced. As soon as we shot the scene, he went back to his trailer and to not speaking to me.

The Re-Worn Dress

For the premiere of my movie at the Tribeca Film Festival in New York, I had on a floor-length, high-neck Jean Muir turquoise wool gown. I was deliberately re-wearing something I'd worn on his *Star Wars* red carpet with the idea that I'd re-wear for my own film events things I'd worn to support him. It may have been then when I understood how frequently I treat my heartbreak as performance art.

In my old dress, it meant a lot to have my old landlord, Scott Caan, by my side. He'd rented me the Laurel Canyon guest house I'd lived in from thirty to thirty-four when I first moved to LA. After my great romantic tragedy of 2010, when he'd hear me sobbing my heart out late into the night, Scott held me as I told him I wished I were dead. He told me that if I felt the same way in a year, he'd personally help me to buy a gun. I didn't feel remotely the same way in a year. Many years later I was alive and Scott came to do one scene in my debut movie.

I told him my marriage was breaking up and that one of the things that weirdly hurt most was that even people who were empathetic couldn't help gasping 'But he's one of the best actors of his generation.'

Scott rolled his eyes. 'Yeah, yeah, come back and talk to me when he's one of the best paediatric cancer specialists of his generation.'

Scott Caan appears in my life once every seven years – like *Brigadoon* – to tell me what I need to hear.

This dress itself had the greatest life. It was originally owned by Gai Pearl Marshall. Gai was Missoni's publicist for forty years and helped to launch Moschino. But before that, she was a Bluebell Girl, and before that, she was a Jewish kid evacuated to Panama during World War Two. This is the great gift of vintage: the energetic power. I love this dress because of the vibrant turquoise of the wool and the fact that it's skintight but covers me neck to foot. But mainly I love it because it was owned by a woman who lived a big life, not just in her youth, but also in middle and old age.

Clothes to Say Goodbye In

Irene Forrest lived to ninety-seven, so her deathbed had been active for a very long time. So long that I'd actually had time to source a funeral-appropriate sleeved, knee-length black Jacques Fath silk dress I bought on a resale website. Online vintage is a gamble and black is particularly high-risk because of how the colour fades over time.

My grandma's hair and skin were fading, too, her face sunken because she was no longer wearing her dentures, her mind diffuse. But when I opened the parcel, this 65-year-old dress was intact. I had it tailored to fit more flatteringly across my hips. My grandma had complained, more than once in my life, that she didn't care for my shape. I think she thought I was using my physique as a form of attention-seeking. The body that is a lighthouse to lovers will always be a headachey neon sign to your Grandma.

But I remember what a lovely conversation we'd had when I called to warn her that I was, the next day, publishing an *Evening Standard* essay about my abortion. My parents had been working to keep the story out of her hands and it bothered me, so I called and told her about it instead, so the secret wouldn't have to be secret.

We talked a long time about her mother, who had died when Grandma was six from a blood infection. 'But,' she said, 'I believe it was a backstreet abortion.'

We talked about her dad, who owned a cinema in the East End of London. My mother's father used to tell her about the weapons they'd fashion in the East End back then, like when someone tried to take his eye out with a flute that had been held over a hot stove.

As it turns out, the last time I saw Irene, I was running off to sign transfer of property papers, wearing a too-short pink vinyl miniskirt with knee socks and a tucked-in T-shirt on which I'd silk-screened Gene Kelly dancing with a mouse. I'd done that for my mum's birthday because she was, like all the kids she knew, so entranced by this sight in the film *Anchors Aweigh* that her local theatre listed not only the showing times, but also the specific time Gene Kelly would dance with the mouse, in case you only wanted to see that.

I looked more attention-seeking than ever, but I don't think Irene could really see me. She talked about the dog she lost sixty-five years earlier, the same year as the dress was made that I'd pre-bought to mourn her. And when I showed her a picture of her favourite film star, Gregory Peck, she smiled. 'That's my husband.' I can easily imagine I'll go out still mourning the beloved pet I lost and believing Gregory Peck was my husband.

Filling the Ache

The floral silver Maison Margiela skirt touched the floor and was my rock bottom, bought online, right before I admitted I'd have to leave my marriage and start a new life. It was a thing of beauty but looked disgusting on me. I'd spent the previous twelve months in a period of compulsive buying, desperately unhappy, determined not to cheat, every item on the internet saying 'take a chance take a chance on me'.

I would never have gone into a shop to look for clothes, because then it would be real: fabrics, tactile, human beings, reason. If the clothes were real, the marriage collapse would feel more real, too. I just wanted to stay afloat, gathering boots and jackets into flotation devices, and as barricades against the door of the room to which I'd lately retreat when I heard his key in the lock.

I can say all of this now because we are both free. But I had to take everything off to get there, holding these items up to the light, hanging them where I could see them as I fell asleep. Figure out what they really meant, what I'd been hoping for each time I'd bought something.

That it coalesced around this skirt is perfect, since it was designed by John Galliano, who had not long earlier been fired and sent to rehab. I have myself been in a twelve-step programme for a few years – you don't need to know which, because they all share the same tenet: that we live in illusion because we're afraid of reality.

Fashion is illusion, as is the advertising of fashion in magazines and on billboards. There is, in those ad campaigns and magazine spreads, a text and also a subtext: if you wear this skirt, you will feel like this . . . But you won't. You won't feel like a carefree young Brigitte Bardot because of a skirt.

Once you can see the subtext, like X-ray spectacles, then what? How do you balance your spiritual awakening with a sincere love of fashion?

In each twelve-step meeting I'd look at women's shoes as I listened. My mother had said, in my darkest times, 'When you wake up, the floor will still be below you and the ceiling will still be above you.' So I tried to have good shoes and good hair, and to look for them in crowds.

But as my marriage was collapsing, the more he drifted from me, the more I bought. I remember a raging fight in the street, him walking away with the baby in her pushchair, leaving me there, wearing a dress I'd only bought to get him to come closer.

Ruffled Deception Dress

This is absolutely as far as you can push a summer day dress: burned orange with buttons down the chest, nipped waist that flares out into a skirt covered in ruffles. I'd had it tailored to my body way back when I lived in New York, in an apartment on 7th Avenue and 13th Street.

Whenever I wore it, I felt powerful like Rita Moreno in *West Side Story*.

The most passionate man I've ever known made love to me as I was wearing it. We knew we only had six hours together, so it didn't feel like there was time to take it off. We were in a hotel suite he'd flown nine hours to reach, just so he could see me before he had to be back at work. I remember how I shook in his arms – literally shook – when he opened the door and kissed me. Shaking because I was between worlds: one foot still in the hall, one half of my body surrendering to him, the other still touched by metro cards, turnstiles, subway stops, Don't Walk signs, rent due, itemised electricity bills. They all went away for six hours and I became whole.

A few years later, the next epic love ripped the dress off me as quickly as he could to get me naked – men want different things, in life and in sex.

I remember the scent of these men. I remember being offered a sample of a cologne in a department store, and how I had to lean against the glass counter and gather myself because it smelled so much of the man from a decade before, in the hotel suite, with the dress still on.

I stayed in my marriage longer than I would have because I was so terrified that people only date through apps now. The thought was unbearable. How can you choose someone if you can't smell them? If you can't first note the fabrics on their body: a surprisingly soft grey sweater that brushes against your bare shoulder blades when he 'accidentally' passes you, clearing the table at a noisy dinner party, but there's only you and him.

Once I have put away these clothes loaded with memories of romance, I move the shoes I haven't worn in a blue moon deep into the attic cupboard. They are gothic former wives not to be mentioned. All ex-wives are crazy, but look at these: pink velvet heels. Red metallic heels. Pale blue leather. What are they for? What are they actually *for*?

This is the subtext I've always seen in fashion campaigns – like *The Manchurian Candidate*, what is it that this fashion editorial is asking me to do? The light on the bare shoulders, the face bare but for kohl eyeliner – oh! they want me to be Brigitte Bardot in Saint-Tropez. OK, I should buy these. Right, now Dolce & Gabbana want me to be Sophia Loren's overflowing body as an antidote to World War Two rationing – we are skipping around here but OK, I'll do that for them. The main thing the shoes do not signify is walking. They are not for protection of human skin from blisters, they are the cause. The pale blue ones, I got married in: they were too confining and so was the marriage.

In fairness, *all* of them are half a size too small. This is perhaps what I returned to the UK to find out after two decades in America. The saying 'you have big shoes to fill' is meant to signal intimidation, but I can see how it's doable – you just keep going. Anyone can walk around in too-big shoes. But to have slightly too-small shoes to fill is infinitely worse.

Wouldn't you want your ex-husband's first girlfriend after your break-up to be beautiful? Oh my God! Is she beautiful. I could not make the marriage work. Because of . . . the shoes. I am my own binding.

I lugged them up the spiral staircase. I can stand up in the loft, and no one else but my daughter and my mother can. It's only that my mother can't climb them any more.

I have a recurring nightmare I have pets I didn't know I owned and when I open the cupboard in the attic and find them, they're almost dead. A few months into the pandemic, worrying I would forget they existed, I went up to check on the shoes. They lay together like the sea lions we saw on a drive to Big Sur. Ben and I were falling apart, but I kept it together because I had been the breadwinner once. Now, he was the breadwinner and was generously paying for my parents to stay at our honeymoon hotel, the Post Ranch Inn. That's why I kept it together – finances and not to break the family bond – and that's the truth, and that's why anyone does it. The Post Ranch Inn does not permit children, so we stayed in our friend's cabin nearby. It was very sad to stay in the loveliest cabin where people in new love would not be able to keep their hands off each other. We kept our distance.

So now I wear wellingtons or trainers and they are all in the attic, these shoes I bought online when I was devastated by my marriage, which happened on a weekly basis. The waves of pain, the shut down, the reaching for the internet. The path of my romantic history is dotted with clothes I bought – they are the Chinese lanterns, the illumination. These shoes are the last part of my former wardrobe now put away.

I have been sexually active since I was sixteen. When I realised how long I had volunteered for a life without sex, I knew I should put these shoes away. I've become suspicious of the high heels, as if they're ancient Egyptian cats, spying for the sun king. I don't live with sun kings any more. And they don't live in me. The biggest, the brightest, the most extreme flamed out and there I said 'enough'. No more sun. Only moon, now. The moon watches through the skylight as I write, makes editorial notes. These shoes, this ghost chorus.

Part Four

Everyone was wanking through lockdown because they were *bored*. But they were also, with the sudden spectre of possible death, exploring their most significant sexual memories. Finding themselves back there, in precise corners and viewed from particular angles but with everything shifting inside – a new take on what had actually been going on that day. Wanking and wanking and wanking about everyone who had ever hurt them, every sexual humiliation and every triumph, and everyone who had ever set them free. The way Buddhists practise for death.

When I reflect on my sexual history, it feels notable that I got one free night at a luxury Hollywood hotel, owing to the fact that when I pulled my underwear on from the floor of the suite, a horde of red ants started stinging my genitals. Still dozy from an afternoon of love-making with a man who had travelled continents to reunite, relishing those hours when you see yourself as they see you, I could not at first fathom the source of this searing pain. I stuck my hand in the Hanes boy pants commonly worn under satin slips by post-feminists in the 2000s and the insects swarmed my fingers. I screamed and ran to the bathroom, and as I sat in the tub, hosing them out, I couldn't stop screaming. The boldest of them had made it into my cervix, and they were as unhappy about it as I. My compadres were my tormenters and I theirs. This would come to feel familiar.

Once I had recovered, I composed myself and went down to the lobby to explain the situation.

'I am so sorry,' said Tony, a concierge who had been tenderly judging me for years.

'The thing is, Tony,' I said, 'a long-distance relationship is hard and this was not helpful.'

I used the tone of voice I'd seen my father model at airports, when passengers were being bumped from flights – he'd not only get us to stay, but he'd also request an upgrade. And that's how I got my complimentary night, as both Tony and his co-workers agreed that, though the hotel is famous for its shenanigans, ants ought not be stinging genitals. Not if the guest hasn't requested that.

I still think of the ants, sometimes, in the bath, as it drains, the horror on my boyfriend's face, how he knew to back out of the room without offering to help. I remember the stinging, and their death. As time passed, the ex retreated somewhere even further than the other side of the globe: he became trapped inside the internet. It was another lifetime and though I've idly googled him once a year, I think of the ants more often than I do him – and it's them for whom I feel a kinship and compassion. They can check out any time they like, but they can never leave.

Then, also, some years after the long-distance boyfriend . . . there was a Nazi in the hotel garden. He was Austrian and when he first floated, uninvited, to the table, to charm me with chat, he name-dropped Princess Michael of Kent. *Then*, in a louder voice, he said Hitler wasn't really a bad guy and he had merely been misconstrued. He had ventured the Princess Michael gambit based on my English accent. But he'd misjudged the second part and when I upbraided him, he said, 'Oh, I see – you are a *Jew*.'

It was upsetting and I got up and told the maître d', who immediately banned him and asked if there was anything else they could do.

I thought about it.

'After a shock it's good to eat sugar, so may I have some dessert? Maybe two or three?'

I have always had an appetite.

Among my sexual memories, there are bad things. A smorgasbord of memories marked 'Best Left Unturned':

Memory One

There's that box of letters that I didn't ever know how to dispose of – letters I'd started receiving when I was fourteen. It took growing up to say, 'If I was fourteen and he was in his thirties, these are not love letters, these are grooming letters.'

I'd sent him a letter, along with a copy of my school newspaper, asking for an interview with one of his clients, which he arranged. Those letters went from box to box, room to room, every place I lived, well into adulthood, not because I treasured them but because they were toxic, waste I hadn't the skill to dispose of.

Someone with an interest in very young people is mis-wired and I was lucky he retreated, didn't force me. After kissing and fondling me in his flat, I said no to the next part. And that was only because I was young enough that it still made me laugh – the idea that *that* could go there, when I saw that it could not. I've googled him. He was and is pathetic, diminished. Whereas I am powerful and likely always was in comparison to such a man.

Eventually, the envelopes ended up in a drawer of a desk in the garage of my Californian marital home. There's black widows and brown recluses in there, spiders pretty common to Southern California. They don't want to be seen – they're scared, too. It doesn't mean they're not frightening.

Memory Two

In the wake of the Harvey Weinstein scandal, a newspaper editor asked me to write my take on Hollywood's #MeToo moment, which she planned to make a cover story. I replied that it was not a comfortable commission for me since I had my own #MeToo story about being a vulnerable sixteen-year-old encountering an abusive man who used to work at that same paper when I was their teenage columnist. In a concerned and respectful email, the editor asked me to come in and talk to her with a company lawyer present. A great therapist told me I didn't have to and it might not help me in any way. That I might feel a lot worse. So I told her, 'No thank you,' and we left it at that.

Memory Three

Because I was so exceptionally young when I was on the scene, I am now medium age, whereas the older men I was involved with are now quite old. I recently walked past one, who was, by a very long shot, the worst in bed and the rudest, the least talented. I was eighteen at the time and he kept saying, as if spectating at horse races, 'Come! Come,' when there was literally nothing either he or I was doing that would have achieved that. In his sixties now, he did not see me, as he was complaining into a mobile phone, on a bus, that he had very bad back ache and depression. The ageing, the collapsing in on itself of the spine and mind are not the punishment I enjoyed for him – rather, it was the talking loudly on a bus about it that seemed just perfect retribution.

When I was a teenager, one man who – and I use my words very carefully here – *had sex with me* is now dead and I know him to have been a very bad man, despite what the obituaries said. What happened between us happened because he was angry at a young girl for being in the same field as him.

I didn't go to sleep afterwards and when it was morning, I left in a cab in pain. It hurt to pee for a week. The interesting part is that I voluntarily kept seeing him for a few weeks. He'd ask me to come over when his wife was out and do things to him, and I would. He gave me a ticket to a music festival as a reward.

This is a story that has come up with several of my friends. One of my dearest went to a bar and woke up in a hotel room tied to a chair, with a man she did not recognise. When he let her go, she gave him her number just so it would not be what it actually was.

I remember who the era's good guys were because they were very few. I've thought of writing to one who is now married with daughters. But I wondered what it would mean to him and whether or not it would merely frighten him. Perhaps it would seem like a threat if I DM'd to say: 'Remember when I was fifteen and you were in your twenties and I said, "No, I don't want to," and you listened and immediately stopped? Thank you?'

Memory Four

When I was sixteen, I made a psychological deal with myself: when this moisturiser I bought at the behest of a woman I was fixated on is finished, I will get over being assaulted by her husband.

The woman never spoke to me again and my fixation on her dissipated with the years – and the shame of the assault with the decades.

I had gone out to San Francisco following her scent after we met at a Breeders concert, where she invited me to visit her if I ever made it to the Bay Area. She was the coolest, the quirkiest-looking, the best-smelling.

I travelled there so far from home because I had so much – too much – freedom. My mother and I agree that now.

'What do you smell of?' I'd asked innocently of my new San Francisco friend as we lay alone on the beach hours after she'd collected me from the airport.

On those coves, I'd posed in my bikini for *her*, but she had sent him to collect the developed photos. When he handed them to her, I noted they'd been opened.

'It's a body moisturiser from this hippy store. I'll take you there and you can have them make you your own bottle!'

So she did.

Later that day, I met her husband and found out there was no spare room, just a fold-out bed in the living room.

And on that very first night, him at the foot of my fold-out bed. Him *in* my fold-out bed. *Twin Peaks*' BOB was a memory so many of us understood: how close he got, how fast he moved, and how time spliced. It didn't happen that night. I lay there, rigid, as if it were normal for a grown man to creep under the covers with you and tell you about their marital problems.

Towards the end of my trip, she was still at work when he took me on a motorbike ride. It was my first time on a motorbike and I was shaking so hard, I almost made us crash. We were on the Golden Gate Bridge and there was nowhere to pull over.

Still shaking with fear when we met her at the bar a while later, I drank way more than I ever had or would have. Way more. Until she could see I was not going to make it through the social night she'd planned with friends. Did she ask him to take me home or did he volunteer? In any case, there was a detour in an alleyway. I did say no, but mainly I was trying not to puke or lose consciousness.

For years, the waves of shame were compounded by the fact that I thought he was good-looking. Anyone with eyes thought he was, because he *was*. But that doesn't mean . . . What doesn't that mean? The shifting interior dreamscape of the teenage girl is her own to control. Nothing ever actually has to happen and that's how the girl stays safe.

Everyone was sad about what happened to Laura Palmer, but they still whispered about her after her demise, the gossip gathering pace with the weeks. Just as it did about me over one night when someone well-meaning took it on themselves to call the rape crisis hotline without my permission and everything snowballed from there.

I could and did heal, but *the wife* was the one I longed for and missed, though no touch beyond a hug had ever passed between us or ever would. It was too late. By the time I landed back in London there were chemtrails of rumour behind me: Did you hear what she was wearing? Why was she even out here all alone? What did she want?

I remember unpacking the tub of handmade body moisturiser and handling it like – this always comes up – kryptonite. Too frightened to use it, it went under the sink in my en-suite. I still lived at home with my parents. Once, I rubbed it on my wrist, but then hurriedly washed it off, as the scent seemed to fill my whole teenage bed-room, staining my posters of the bands Blur and Pulp, these clever, weak men, sitting beside the Sophia Loren and Lauren Bacall glossies. Both Bacall and Loren chose, very young, to marry older protectors and then to stay with them until they died, letting men want them but always having an older guardian to stop them from get-ting too close. Why didn't you choose that the moment you got breasts? Stupid girl. Stupid, stupid girl.

It hits me only now as I write these sentences: I had my honeymoon in the place I fractured? Did I subconsciously make the connection when I suggested the road trip to Ben? Was I hoping his alpha male presence would sanctify the past?

When a year after that first trip to San Francisco you check on the handmade moisturiser, it has turned bad, and decades later, when you check on it in your head, you can still smell both scents so strongly (how it was when it was purchased and how it was when the scent turned). Though you can smell them in your dreams, you still can't describe them. Maybe that's why you just get married one day, instead. In lieu of, and as payment for, indescribable teenage scents.

The man with his motorbike is gone. I have no picture of him in my head. Not his face, not his body and certainly not his scent. He probably looked like an actor you'd hire as a last-minute replacement if your real male lead dropped out.

Every girl and woman has a story like this. I landed at the luckier end of the scale, of this I am well aware.

I wonder where my life would have gone if it had been her and not him who had crawled into my bed that first night. I've never yearned for women more than any other ostensibly heterosexual woman does, I don't think.

Is this true? It is men I desire sexually but women are my romance, my fascination. Why would you queue in any gallery to look at a painting of a man? How could you ever sit through the whole two hours and thirty-six minutes of *The Revenant*, with some men, and a bear, and some reven-ing? I get uneasy without women to look at or listen to, even on a short bus ride.

It was a long, long time ago, a wormhole really – a different kind from lockdown but a wormhole nonethe-less . . .

I do remember what she smelled like.

And how I travelled across the world, age sixteen, to inhale her.

When I was a girl, both parents working full-time and our house being renovated, we had a nanny who threatened: 'If you misbehave, I will let the builders watch you in the bath.' She was in her late teens. She never followed through, but the threat, and the effect she knew it would have, are the reason I've only ever hired childminders in their fifties and sixties, stable grandmother figures. She wrote to congratulate me after the publication of my first novel, unaware that her threat remains a scratch in my psychic vinyl.

In the early days of one relationship, I'd sometimes climb out of my boyfriend's bed and open his laptop to look at pornography sites bookmarked in his history as an odd way of trying to feel closer to him. One dawn, I came back to bed shaking so badly it woke him. I confessed what I'd been doing and that this time I'd seen – on the sidebar of offerings that pop up, unwanted, like chyrons on a cable news channel – a video of a girl I was sure was underage. My boyfriend sat up 'That happens sometimes, and it makes me very angry.'

I thought about our desires and how close they can bump against far darker places. She returns to me sometimes – if I'm stressed or sleepless – this underage girl from the pop-up, and the memory makes me feel sicker and more broken than anything I've actually been through.

There was one positive male figure during that time, and I will always remember him.

I was sixteen and had made it into a secret Beastie Boys album launch concert in the tiny, damp basement of the skateboarding brand Slam City Skates. I was 5 foot 1 and always would be but I didn't know it then – I was still waiting for more to come. Although I had what I now recognise as a jaw-dropping body, I was dressed in a way that conspired against my form – the sweet teenage-girl stupidity of dressing like the men you are attracted to, in this case Liam Gallagher, as if Jessica Rabbit had only ever gone out in an oversized cagoule – my hair a triangle of curls as parched as my heart. I was the same shape as teenage Elizabeth Taylor, but she hadn't been a teen in the aftermath of Madchester and she had MGM Studios sew her into a tight gown the second she got her epic breasts. I was . . . I was a mess.

I did not feel very desirable and, like all teenage girls, was dumb enough to repeat that out loud.

And then he was beside me, long, elegant bassist fingers, almost but not quite touching my face, as he softly said, 'Pleiades.'

Adam Yauch, aka MCA, the prematurely grey member of the Beastie Boys, the quiet, thoughtful George Harrison of the band, the one who had found Buddhism, started the Tibetan Freedom Concerts and nudged the band to atone for their early days of sexism, had noticed me.

'What?' I asked.

'Pleiades. The constellation? The freckles under your left eye are in the shape of Pleiades. It's *so* beautiful.'

If I'd known a way to keep talking, he would have. But I didn't, so he smiled and let himself be pulled away, looking back at me.

Maybe that brief spotlight, from a man who had been gentle, encouraging and romantic but non-lascivious, planted my love for the stars and moon. But it bloomed wildly, when I turned forty, five novels in, one young daughter, waiting for the divorce papers to be signed.

Hiking with my headphones on, I've noticed that stars must be the second most referenced imagery in popular music, after the heart. The heavens were, of course, singer David Bowie's muse, walking alongside him from young 'Starman' until the album released the day before he died: *Blackstar*. In later life, Bowie was asked if he'd like to go to the moon now Virgin were selling tickets. 'I wouldn't dream of [it] . . . I'm scared going down to the end of the garden.' The moon and stars were his Superman costume.

I understand this completely and wonder if I ended up living in LA so long because it is a city of stars on stars: the arc of the constellations reflect the endless lights of Mulholland, reaching up to them as if they were lovers torn apart. It is hypnotic.

I started seriously monitoring the moon when my marriage was in freefall. I'd had a blue-grey veil, an orange almond cake and two wedding dresses. One that bound me tight all the way up my neck for the religious ceremony – following negotiations with the rabbi about adding material that would cover all of my tattoos – and one for wild dancing. It was only looking back on my wedding photos that I saw I'd also had a full moon that night. I'd worked so hard and long to save my marriage, it blew my mind that you can't fight or thwart the moon. It won't be persuaded. You are powerless.

How much courage that realisation gave me ... I'd always fantasised about living in a hotel, so that each day, when I came back to a room made tidy, I'd have a fresh chance to get things right. The cycle of the moon is an endless begin again. The ultimate reset peace offering.

It is solidly reliable – same time, same place every month – while also sexy. That's rare. That, right there, is the dream lover. I'll see you same time, same place every month, and I'll make you feel crazy and free.

After the divorce, relocated to London, on a bus passing through North London suburbs, I saw, in a shop window, a print of a woman kissing a man made out of stars. Everything fell into place. In a capitalist society approaching endgame, it's come to feel like only stars and orgasms offer free pleasure. I saw that print and had the strong sense that my greatest love affairs have involved being in places where the stars and moon were most visible. A secret Auckland beach in New Zealand. A remote Irish clifftop.

People have been watching the stars, living by them, loving by them for thousands of years, which puts our personal sorrows into perspective. My first epic love was a Maori – he came from people who had navigated from Hawaii to New Zealand by the stars. My kid doesn't understand why I cry so hard when we get to the song 'We Know the Way' from her favourite Disney film, *Moana*. That while we are having mother–daughter bonding, I am overcome with a bittersweet erotic pang.

The first thing we did, all three of us, as a family post-divorce filing was go and see *Moana*. Ben rocked back and forth, both palms clutching his face as tears coursed down his cheeks and we let him – and afterwards didn't ask about it. I knew he was thinking of the grandma who had taken him in when neither parent could handle him. And I wept when Moana approaches the terrifying monster, arms outstretched, and the monster becomes beautiful. I was crying about him – he was crying about how he'd become him. Our kid was just laughing at Maui, the God of Mischief.

Because of that first epic love, Maui is now on my left wrist. I couldn't leave behind his scent and I travelled extensively through the Polynesian triangle. In Hiva Oa, the island tattoo artist etched me with Maui.

As for astrology (the divination of human affairs by studying the movement of celestial objects), well, sure, it's a bullshit pseudoscience, but it also predates religion. Anything that has been believed by that many people for that long inevitably holds a power. You don't need to believe it's real. But you can accept there's power in so many people believing. It is, in that sense, like conventional religion, to which I have also been drawn as an adult.

In my twenties, in love in New Zealand, there was that sense of being cradled by the sky. I'm shocked, in retrospect, how clearly that was not the case from the lover and I wonder if I confused the sky with him. It stepped in where he was incapable. The respite from his emotional absence was the nights he'd make love to me in that pickup truck on the beach, our neurotic constellations melding.

In my thirties, new lover: Ireland, again those epic stars, the euphoric amplification of our nascent feelings so we were wildly in love before we'd spent any length of domestic time together.

My life is all domestic now. I fall asleep every Sunday night listening to my favourite astrology show, the host beaming possible pathways from her garden office in Oakland, California to my new life in North London. 'I love that question,' she always tells callers. 'I cannot tell you how much I love that question.' In a world that feels black-and-white, good and evil, it is comforting to delve into astrology – a world in which everything is constantly open to interpretation.

I live on top of a hill, in this little top-floor flat I bought because it felt old and decrepit and suffused with the magic of its endless view. The further my romantic life has receded (something beautiful and strange, much too far away to touch), the more I've been drawn to the stars. With their Greek names they are my Greek chorus, helping me to process the story of my life as it continues to unfold.

I think I'd miss sex more if I didn't have the sensual pleasure of the moon gazing at me, the stars running themselves over my body as I moon bathe in my underwear on my roof terrace on a warm night. Instead of a farmer's tan, I feel constellations drifting into my hair like snow.

An after-effect of having known so much passion is, now I am alone, that I feel passionate about the night stars. And I get turned on when I look up in the shower and see, through the skylight, fast-moving clouds on blue sky. Why are they so fast? Who are they racing towards? When there's no human lover, the whole Earth feels erotic. If I spent money now, it wouldn't be on more clothes, it would be on expanding the skylight, so I could see even more of the stars when I'm in the bath.

No one can ever touch me without my consent again. I consent only to the stars.

Here is another man . . . who was a good man, not a bad man:

Marc Spitz had the same name as the nine-time Olympic swimming champion and the haircut of a Roman emperor, but his physicality was closer to comedian Bill Hader's Stefon character from *Saturday Night Live*. As we talked, he'd touch his face with the fingertips of both hands, bit by bit, as if blotting spilled ink. Marc was a great rock journalist and a good playwright, and he had a lot of friends in both high and low places who loved him, but he was his own spilled ink.

For our debut novels we shared the same editor, who introduced us during a literary salon at the KGB Bar in the East Village, New York. I really notice the north and south in London, but over ten years in New York, it was only east and west that were my delineators, since it would not occur to me to go above 14th Street. The only reason I'd do so was to take the subway once a week to my shrink and, when I did, I'd emerge blinking and terrified of the WASPish older ladies (Upper East Side) and older gentlemen with waspish humour (Upper West Side).

I arrived late to the literary salon, in jeans and an off-the-shoulder floral crop top such as Linda Ronstadt might wear for a hot date in 1973. I'd just purchased and worn it out from a vintage store next to The Pink Pony diner on Ludlow Street. I loved the way that vintage stores, like diners, always seemed to be open late in New York – they went hand in hand to me, both representing the triumph of a fresh start in the face of lived experience. Geographically, they seemed to cluster together, the desire for one feeding into the other. Me, diners and vintage stores were the only threesome I've ever had, but one that happened a lot.

Marc seemed to come from way more money than I did but had a lot less of it. His sexuality also puzzled me. Today, he would probably be described as non-binary, but then it was just called being a Jewish male.

'I like him,' I explained to my mum. 'I mean I would, maybe, have been interested romantically, but I mean . . . look?'

I showed her a Polaroid I'd taken of him in his regular uniform of Jackie O sunglasses and feather boa.

'Oh!' said Mum after the briefest glance. 'That's just Jewish men. They're forever looking for reasons to put on dresses.'

Really? What about John Garfield playing the tough guy in all the noir movies I'd been watching? And what of Mark Spitz, the actual Olympic swimmer with the same name?

'Mum, are you sure? Isn't that English men you're describing?'

'Well, yes. *Monty Python* and all that. Yes, both.'

My father being an English Jew, I think I elected then that I would marry a *binary* man. So I wasn't attracted to Marc. But I was always drawn to him.

Living streets apart in Greenwich Village, I used to meet him at odd hours at the 24-hour diner whose name I would never forget but that I've now forgotten. Eating grape jelly on toast in the dead of night while Marc wrote mix tapes on the paper tablecloth. I knew Aaron Sorkin wrote the script for *A Few Good Men* on paper napkins. Marc never made it as a writer like Aaron did, but I found his mix tapes more emotionally resonant.

No one had ever played me 'Another Girl, Another Planet' by The Only Ones. It lit me up so much that, after I heard it, I let Marc put his fingers inside me, even though that wasn't what I was after and neither, frankly, was he. We never mentioned it. That was the only night we ever made out. Perfunctory and polite, it could only disappoint in comparison to our midnight ambitions and mix tapes.

He'd ring my bell because he was passing, or I'd ring his. In adulthood, that is like a nightmare – an unannounced visitor – but then it was part of the sell of NYC, that you could at any hour receive a drop-in from a friend. He often DJ'd at The Slipper Room, and a set featuring Hall & Oates and Cheap Trick would be preceded by a reading from one of Marc's plays by a pre-*Game of Thrones* Peter Dinklage.

But mainly, we'd meet at the Library Bar on Hudson. Sunglasses and scarf in place, Marc would move his hands through his pockets at the bar, like a mime, until you paid for the round. I told him about the neighbour whose music I'd heard through the chimney, and how I'd walked upstairs and knocked on his door. The next day the neighbour had left a mix CD on my doormat, which I now sought Marc's help in parsing, since the neighbour had not tracklisted it.

Marc identified each song, nodding in grudging approval or sighing in annoyance. One particularly beautiful alt-country song began with the line: 'Devastation at last finally we meet.'

'What is this?' I asked Marc. 'Why has he done this?'

He identified it as 'Mockingbirds' by Grant Lee Buffalo and waved his long fingers dismissively.

'Oh! that's just a song men put at the end of mix tapes to make themselves seem sensitive.'

One day, as punishment or a test – they tend to merge at that age – I made Marc go into the Christopher Street photo developers to collect naked New Zealand ocean photos my on–off boyfriend had taken of me. They were breathtaking. My waist was twenty-three inches, my hips closer to forty, and I'd had a reaction to contraception, so my 32F breasts stood out like shelves, the way only small breasts usually do. I was twenty-five and truly resembled the Jewish Jessica Rabbit, if that's what anyone was looking for – which I guess the Polynesian lover was.

Marc handed over the pictures, looking bored. If they in any way piqued his interest, he didn't let on behind his Jackie O glasses.

(The photos were taken by the same Polynesian man who had caused me to find ants in my pants. He kept trying to break up with me and, when I called my mum, weeping, my mum said to tell him he wasn't allowed to break up with me – so I did, and that worked? It worked but wasn't the best advice. In terms of life. But she was pissed off about all the constant drama.)

I kept flying to New Zealand for him – he'd show up in New York and make me cry. One night, at dinner, as I spun out and wailed over this man, Marc recalled that the highest charting record by a Polynesian act was 'How Bizarre' by OMC. When I finally came up for breath – weeping about how tragic and sick it was that he would come back to try to repair our relationship a week after I had the abortion he'd pointed me towards – Marc merely sighed, drew on the napkin and murmured: 'How bizarre.'

It made me feel a lot better. It always makes me feel better at times of operatic pain to be made fun of. It makes me feel considerably better than being empathised with. I guess that's the English in me – the same part that loves Erasure, Soft Cell and The Beautiful South. It makes me smile to write about Marc, after hours, when I might have walked over there to stay the night in his studio apartment, us un-touching but listening to each other breathe. Now, I'm up because I fell asleep at a weird angle in a single bed trying to get my daughter to sleep.

At a Blur concert, late into our friendship, right before I left New York for LA, Marc put his arms around my shoulders and said, 'Emma? I love you.'

'No you don't,' I said, laughing. 'You're just leaning on me because I'm small and you're tall.'

'I do!' Then he paused . . . 'I love you late at night, when you're far away.'

I agreed that was fair enough, this was a sentiment I understood. It was very 'Another Girl, Another Planet'. We could still be friends because Marc was just being *Marc*.

I miss that New York life of strolling from point a to point b, with so many possible things happening on the way, where I'd become close with a man I met at a literary salon because we were both walkable and mutable.

At some point, Marc acquired a young girlfriend named Lizzy, a music journalism hopeful I was a little intimidated by. Because no one had ever been younger than me in my field and yet there she was, nineteen to my twenty-five.

Marc and I had drifted not only emotionally, but also geographically by the time he suddenly died. A few years after his death, Lizzy Goodman – who had stayed his girlfriend but become thirty-five – invited me to lunch in LA. We'd never been alone before, but then Marc had always been alive before. She looked so powerful as a grown woman, with killer cheekbones and straight stripes of turquoise liner under each eye. I found her very warm and I felt warm for her success.

She was sorry to hear of my divorce and told me to set up a dating app. I replied that the idea of meeting someone on an app horrified me and was part of the reason I'd stayed in my marriage longer than I'd intended, aware this was now the way of the world. She insisted I download it, not necessarily to use it, but just as a way to tell the universe I was open to meeting someone one day. She showed me how to do it and there the app sat on my touch screen, untouched, for some time.

Back in the day, I'd lain on a bed with Marc, holding hands and not having to do anything else, because one of us was their own spilled ink, and the other was out of fountain pen cartridges and hadn't noticed. Maybe, if he were here, we'd stare at the ceiling of my bedroom and I'd say to him, 'My ex-husband's new girlfriend is twenty-one.' And he'd say, 'So what, you're still hot.' Then I'd add, 'She's also Brazilian.' And he'd press his face with his fingertips and say, 'Oh yeah. That's bad. I'd feel really insecure if I were you.'

Pauly Fuemana, the singer-songwriter who was OMC, died young and fragile, too, after leaving behind poverty in New Zealand via 'How Bizarre', only to return to it, a broken one-hit wonder.

So the jokes weren't funny, after all. Or maybe they still are. Everything's funny, so long as it's 3 a.m. at a 24-hour diner, or you're late at night and far away.

Now, I write in the attic of my top-floor flat on top of a hill. This is what it feels like to be celibate after divorce, in the middle of a lockdown. It feels peaceful. The space is small but the view is huge. Being celibate in that flat on top of a hill was the first time I felt myself looking outwards and inwards, simultaneously.

I have often watched the men closest to me retreat as a means of protection – when they feel threatened or when something is beyond their understanding. I remember my dad not speaking to my mother, my sister or me for a whole day after noticing my first tattoo on a beach holiday. He just wouldn't speak to us and we didn't know why.

A few times a month, my husband would go three days without speaking to me, walking in and out of rooms without acknowledging my presence, dark glasses on in the house as a warning not to get close to him. I'd follow him room to room pleading, 'What did I do?' The visceral gratitude I'd feel when the silence was lifted – it didn't matter that I didn't know why I'd been forgiven or what for.

But post-divorce, we have shared the house many times and I always let him go quiet until he isn't. I never ask what it's about, let alone if it's to do with me. This has been in tandem with my own inner quiet. I describe it as inner quiet, but forgoing the touch of other human beings has brought me single-note sounds of great clarity – long-sustained notes like Bill Withers singing 'Lovely Day'.

The best writing ideas are often after the orgasms I deliver myself in the stillness. Sometimes reading other people's writing makes me need to come. Sometimes the process of writing my own does, too. The attic flat I bought is hyper-feminine. Where once I lived inside my own broken heart, I now live inside my own womb.

From the attic, I tried to pre-order my annual lunar diary planner, shipping it to the marital home because the Californian company didn't send abroad. But there seemed to be a glitch in the system. I re-entered it. Then understood. I'd misremembered my old address. That house that meant everything to me? This was the first time it had happened, not remembering where I lived, and I like that it's connected to a pre-order – the future isn't fixed and nor, it seems, is the past.

Getting to middle age has been a process of learning, knowing, believing. Proving that the words of the children at school about you were not true. That the words of the man you worshipped when you were a teen were not true. He told you you were a good fit for each other because you were both unattractive. He was wrong. It was only him who was ugly. You moved to America and got told you were beautiful, and sorry, but you can't unsee it. Whether or not it is objectively true, you learned to believe it. Now what? Having finished that painstaking excavation, what do you use the next half of your life for?

You were a detective. You took your leads about yourself, impatient for a break in the case. When it came to discovering who you were, you acted both as renegade gumshoe and double-crossing dame. Until you got your moment. You broke the case! You are free.

I'll sometimes see a palm tree in suburban London and catch myself crying, missing LA. I try to feel out what exactly I'm missing. I think I'm missing magic. I think I miss the sense of the universe being out of my hands. I do have less sense of that here, because we don't have brush fire, landslide or earthquake season. The more concise Britishness can trick you into terrible responsibility that things are in your control. But rest assured, landslide or no landslide: it's out of your hands.

My daughter asks again, has asked a few times lately: 'When was the nearest time something was from the olden days?' I say, 'Punks!' Because I remember seeing them everywhere when I was a kid. So my childhood is the most recent time something was olden days.

I have a photo of me, her age, among Trafalgar Square punks you could pay to take a Polaroid with. I am small, olive, both hopeful and sad, wise beyond my years but out of my depth. Nothing ever changed.

As I put her to bed in her London bunk, trying not to drift into her sleep with her, I thought back to that night in LA so long ago, when the candles twinkled in the magic-hour hotel garden that Jack Cardiff used to make the golden-age beauties more beautiful. I remembered

Part Five

All of the bad sex stuff happened exclusively in my youth – that's what they value and that's when they can steal from you. Of course, terrible sex things can happen to a woman at any age, but it is not routine the way it is for young women.

There is so much shame. So much that shouldn't have happened to me, not at any age, but especially not then, tied as it was to the initial wave of finding success as a writer. I get such terrible shocks in life, over and over again. Many of the things *were* shocking – anyone would be rattled by them, especially a young girl. But much of what followed, of what still follows, are things a person who took less damage could shake off and get on with their day after. I took heed of my Sophia Loren and Lauren Bacall posters, and I sought and found a tough husband who barked at strangers, to keep the frightening things in my head at bay that had bothered me since I began to become a woman.

Once, foolishly, I told him that my sister and I considered Paul Reiser in *Mad About You* to be the ideal husband. There followed, in time, a discussion that devolved into him shouting, 'I'll never be your Paul Reiser! I'll never be Mandy Patinkin! You chose the wrong kind of Jew! I'm not ever going to be some mild beta male!'

And I thought, it's true, Ben must come from the same line as Bugsy Siegel and Meyer Lansky, as I hissed, 'Mandy Patinkin is *not* mild.'

And he shouted, 'I was referring to Paul Reiser.'

And I muttered that it had not been clear, and he spat he *had* been clear but that I am *eristic*. I wanted to google 'eristic' but I was too upset.

I'm not upset about it any more.

(It means argumentative as well as logically invalid.)

In every city I've lived, my sister has been the one to set up the printer, testing it by printing me the lyrics to George Michael's 'Freedom! '90'. I am not the only grown woman entwined with their family, as I am not the only Brit entwined with George Michael. When, in 2010, he drove his car through the wall of the Hampstead Heath Snappy Snaps, the resulting hole was quickly daubed with the legend 'WHAM' by a local who meant it in a loving way. Walking to the Tube, I saw it (the aftermath and the commentary on the aftermath) after a breakfast with the last man I dated before I met my husband.

Because I'd seen his film (*Animal Kingdom*), and he'd read my book (*Your Voice in My Head*), Ben and I had a strong idea of each other before we fell in love. Once we were together, music moved from headphones in walking cities to being blasted from his truck on LA highways.

My soon-to-be husband began a rapid career ascendancy as he endeavoured, simultaneously, to untangle me from my family. As we worked on the wording to our Ketubah (Judaism's sacred prenuptial agreement) I could picture beside '. . . according to the law of Moses and Israel,' the calligraphed lyrics to 'Freedom! '90':

> I won't let you down
> I will not give you up!

Though I'd left home at sixteen, it felt, in many ways, as if it was only just happening. On hearing me plead my case to my father as to why I shouldn't have to invite a relative I didn't like to the wedding, Ben took the phone from me. I heard my dad, in clipped John Cleese tones, politeness enveloping a core of near demented frustration.

'It may not be pleasant, but you have to. We had to invite family we didn't want to our wedding – it's just how weddings work.'

'Ah, *nah*, *mate*,' Ben answered, fanning out his Aussie accent like a card trick. '*Nah*. That ain't gonna happen.' And he hung up on him.

Like many families from minority ethnic backgrounds, mine is loud. Here was someone who was far louder.

But DMX is loud and Cher is also loud, and they're different. And you'd be resentful on marrying if your concept of how loudness should feel was one and you got the other.

> May not be what you want from me
> Just the way it's got to be . . .

My husband was an Australian male who treated me like an English rose (the man who brushes me with his backpack at San Francisco airport's baggage claim is admonished, 'Get *away* from my wife!'). I had only been a wife for forty-eight hours and Ben kept saying the word out loud as if testing a key in a lock. I did the same on that honeymoon road trip, saying 'husband' each time we woke in a new bed.

The absolute apex of my love for Ben was, when he did not like a much-lauded film, rather than saying, 'I find I am not connecting with this jazz drummer's emotional journey', he instead ejected the DVD, spat on it, opened the window, threw the DVD out, closed the window, then opened the window and leaned out to spit on it again.

One of the lows was me trying to finish a breastfeeding session with our three-week-old and him playing 'Wild for the Night' by ASAP Rocky feat. Skrillex over and over from tinny laptop speakers turned to their highest volume. Thereafter, I came to imagine that any vile event in our marriage featured Skrillex. But that day, topless and trapped under my suckling infant, I simply spat as far as I could in the direction of the laptop. The spit landed on the keyboard.

'Oh my God,' shouted Ben, 'I love you! I love you so much!'

Did he love my anger, my focus, my aim? I don't think he knew why he loved me, just that we had a primal connection. I felt the same. I followed his scent from room to room.

Nor is it lost on me that the heights of our love are both to do with spit. I think about the English phrase 'holding it together with spit and glue', which is another way of saying hanging on by a thread. We hung by a thread for years.

'You're shouting!' I'd cry. 'You're scaring me!'

And he'd answer, 'I'm not shouting. I'm Australian. You're scared of everything!'

He still thinks I am too easily startled and I still think he is scary. This is the circle in which we dance and always did. You deliberately chose as a husband a man so dominant and loud he could scare away all of your bad memories. And then you notice that you get scared of him? It's like realising that your cat's breath smells of cat food.

But we were in motion, with a sense that going off-piste could, itself, lead to destruction.

My husband had studied early childhood back in therapy and he kept telling our baby, as she clung to me, her eyes following me around the room: 'You can have her for now. When you are three years old, I'm gonna take her back.' He said it to her over and over, but it was for me to understand, a reassurance. That this distance that inevitably springs between a couple following childbirth would end. It would not always be me and her a unit, he an adjoining granny flat. Until then, he gave us space and slept downstairs.

She'd wake five times a night in her cot. If I just let her sleep in the bed with me, she'd sleep through. When he joined us, he'd keep getting up to smoke, or at 6 a.m. he'd start using the coffee grinder and blasting AC/DC. This had been touching as a new couple, the restlessness, that energetic pull, a strange current I would surrender willingly to.

Maybe things would have been different if she hadn't been born with a mass of dark hair that held all of his cigarette smoke to it with all the closeness a baby girl wants from her father. I asked him to shower before he lay down with us, but that made him feel bad. And with the years, I understand both of our perspectives. The importance of how someone smells in wanting to be close to them. So he just started sleeping downstairs. How new dads do. But also how trolls under bridges do.

'I am not,' he said at the end, 'prepared to be your monster any more.'

I had my placenta turned into pills in an attempt to ward off post-natal depression. I had an acupuncturist come to the house the first weekend home from hospital to attempt the same. For one month, while recovering from the C-section, I took the last of my savings and spent it on a baby nurse, who arrived at 7 p.m. and left at 7 a.m. Ben was as upset as I'd ever seen him. He didn't think I should have had a C-section and he hated me having a baby nurse. 'I wanted us to do this together.' He said my decision to do this against his wishes was unilateral and steamrolling. I said it was my money, my birth and my recovery. That though I had not had a mental health flare in many years, it felt like a trapdoor in my brain and I wanted the extra protection.

After the baby nurse moved on, I interviewed nannies, until I found the right lady to work seven hours a day, Monday to Friday.

Una is a grandmother from Kingston, Jamaica. She wore a special hat to the interview and said, 'But she's cute!' when she saw CJ, later explaining that you don't expect a white baby to be cute.

'How long is she staying?' Ben asked.

'Well, she is our nanny.'

'So, for how many weeks?'

'Um. For the ageing of the baby into a toddler and then a child?'

It dawned on me, a little too late, that this had never come up. It had all moved so fast. I had assumed we'd have childcare, as my mother had for us when she was working full-time. He said he assumed I'd write whenever the baby was sleeping.

Imagine not knowing until after your baby was born that there was an expectation there would be no childcare.

'But . . . but I'm a writer.'

'I thought,' he said again, 'we were going to do this together.'

And so instead of a first-month glow, he was furious at me.

It is true my desires were bigger than our living space. If you were a man upset by the presence of a nanny and sought to avoid her, it was going to be hard.

Una was great at picking around our emotional messiness.

That baby was sparkling clean, too.

'Let all of your troubles and worries float away with the water,' Una would say as she washed the baby's hair.

I looked into CJ's little eyes to see what her troubles might be, but they weren't really focusing yet, not the eyes, nor the troubles. Mine were very focused: I was scared of dropping her, of her rolling off something, but mainly I was terrified of washing her hair because there was so much of it.

I knew she'd been born because the doctor squealed, 'That's the most hair I've seen on a baby in a long time!'

Then they put her on my chest and I said, 'Isn't she lovely!'

Which was the song my dad had tried to request at our wedding but had been crying too hard to get the words out.

All babies born with a lot of hair look like used-car salesmen, but that never occurred to me. To me, CJ's hair was Disney level in length and mystical powers. So much responsibility. It fitted in the same psychic terror space as learning how to drive. There could be serious ramifications for other human beings if I got this wrong.

Una might have been able to wash baby hair, but she also could not drive and, like me, was terrified of learning in LA. She was driven every day from the valley by her husband, Johnny, who then went home and came back for her in the evening. It took us a long time to coax him inside.

'Mate!' said Ben. Then, 'Maaate!'

But he would not budge.

The pair had met in Kingston, when Johnny stopped her then boyfriend from attacking her at the airport.

Una explained, 'You are not allowed to do that there. They're very proud of Kingston Airport.'

One of the last vacations we took before the pandemic shut down the world was to Jamaica to attend Una's sixtieth birthday. Everyone was instructed to wear white and I wore a white Hanes boy tank top, white linen pants and white Converse. I realised the mistake I had made when I saw the other guests looking like they were going to the

Grammys and *Vanity Fair*'s Oscar Party and a royal christening. So many heels, so many hats. Mink false eyelashes and fabulous acrylic nails.

Una entered in colour, an inspiration she got from a rap video. A singer sang 'Wind Beneath My Wings' and her family had to hold her upright because she was collapsing with emotion. It was one of the best parties I've ever been to. That's before the toasts even began.

CJ looked out at the assembled ladies.

'Una used to look after me. She was kind.'

And they thought that was very sweet.

I saw CJ look out at her audience, process the gradations of brown skin and huge hats. Her mental Rolodex was visible to me as she flipped straight to *RuPaul's Drag Race*, stuck her chubby palm in the air and bellowed to the crowd: 'Can I get an amen up in here?' There was silence for just a beat before the assembled hat ladies lost it.

One day, when CJ had just been born and Una had just arrived, I got it together to walk a few blocks up the road. Towards Fred Segal, as if pointed towards Mecca, the billboard as triggering for those invested in LA mythology as the Chateau Marmont sign. I was leaking and lolloping. On my way back, I saw one of the few men on Earth with whom I've had a one-night stand – the comedian who had texted me late one night when I was reading *The New York Times* obituary page. A successful one-night stand because it became three nights.

I like tall men for the same reason I like California: I like to feel small in the world; for there to be an expanse above me to dream into – it is part of experiencing awe. This man had that kind of tall that made it look like his skin had shrunk a size in the wash. In the bedroom, so beautiful. But now his tall just made me notice him in a twenty-minute space I was craving solitude. I didn't want to see him and he didn't want to see me like this.

In that moment, I felt the shame of my body as a working machine rather than an instrument of pleasure. The father of my child can see me this way – when I'm ready, when I've consented – but not a one-night stand when I'm not expecting it. *Fuck.*

I'd had a tailor make me a few beautiful pre- and post-partum jumpsuits – a terrible idea and it's right there in the name: I don't want to jump, I've just had a baby, I can barely walk. So I was trying to walk in an ill-judged jumpsuit, when the comedian saw me and did the polite thing, which is pretend he *hadn't* seen me – and for this, at least, I was grateful. But . . .

I wonder if that was the very first step – before I knew what I was doing, before I decided to be celibate by choice – into not being seen by men. My gratitude at being ignored sending the universe quite the wrong message.

The friends Ben made while shooting *The Place Beyond the Pines* were my favourite to be around in post-partum vulnerability. I had particular soft spots for Tom the dialect coach, Derek the director, and Ryan, the star, who hauled our heavy changing table up the stairs to the baby's nursery because he'd got his professional mover's licence for his role in *Blue Valentine.*

These were Hollywood people, only not. They just wanted to make art and each of them asked me about mine – before, during and after pregnancy. That was so rare and so welcome. When Derek visited from Brooklyn and asked me about my next book, it hit me how long it had been since someone in our LA work orbit had wondered.

Then the financial change came fast. In Big Sur, Ben had promised he'd get rich, and he did. A few years later, we were sat on the same table as the tall one-night stand at a function. In this context, I simply cannot be ignored.

I have got myself together, I probably look good enough, if too excited to be outdoors. I was smiling, unjudging, cheery. I wanted everything to be OK. Everything was awkward, from every single angle.

I have never desired one-night stands. In fact, the few times I've experienced them I've been left with that unhappy feeling you get after craving chocolate but only getting your hands on something from a service station that is so watered down, it might as well be made from chickens' eyelashes as cocoa.

I only want exciting sexual experiences, so I choose exciting men because that seems like a reasonable bet. And that has worked out. But . . . they are mad.

Like the tall one-night stand. When I went to his home – a huge, empty mansion – the only framed picture I could see was a looming portrait of Peter Sellers. Wouldn't you keep your clothes on and leave? But I stayed there, took off my clothes and all but shrieked, 'Watch *this*, Peter Sellers!'

So you cannot say, not right before you walk up the aisle, 'Just wanted to check quickly. Sorry I didn't have the courage to ask this before, because I was really enjoying being in love with you, but: do you know that you are mad?'

Because that would be like telling a vampire that you know they're a vampire. Then they'd have to destroy you. So, you don't say it and get slowly destroyed instead – with an enormous amount of pleasure and laughter along the way.

Many years pass and you *still* don't ask: 'Did you know you are mad?' And then you are divorced and have a six-year-old child whose father replies, when she asks if – having seen it pastiched on *The Simpsons* – she can watch *A Clockwork Orange*, 'Absolutely not!' Then mails her a *Clockwork Orange* jigsaw puzzle of Malcolm McDowell having his eyelids peeled back in their sockets, since she is not allowed to watch the actual movie for twelve more years. She nurtures the awful visual like a precious thing because it is from him and he has tried very hard, in his way, to meet her needs.

And it's OK because you're mad too. And, most importantly, your parents are still mad *and* still together coming on fifty years because their neuroses fit like a jigsaw puzzle. That was the template for the coming together of you and Ben. It's just that yours don't fit. And even if they did, neither of you would have the patience to work on a fucking jigsaw puzzle long enough to find out.

My husband was so furious with me one night that, before he retreated to the guest bedroom, he hissed, 'You can't drive. You can't cook. All you can do is write and fuck, and you can't even do that any more.'

He wasn't wrong. I mean, I was devastated, but I also thought, well, he really gets me.

Usually, when things were at a particularly bad ebb between us, he'd leave to go and shoot a film – or maybe we steered things to a bad ebb because we were upset about him leaving to go and shoot a film. I often suspected it was the latter. I attempted to paper over the deep cracks by working on the surface. After he left, I made an effort to recover my body.

Having done so, I'd gone on the 218 bus to the sale at Nordstrom, the luxury department store, with the baby attached to me, where I picked out an expensive pair of new trousers, much reduced. To try them on, I laid CJ down on the dressing-room floor and hoped the thirty-second rule about food also applied to babies.

They were blue silk with a grey stripe up the side, cut in that very wide style of Katharine Hepburn. Before childbirth, at my fittest, I'd been shaped like Salma Hayek, short and curvy. Forgetting your own previous body type is classic baby brain. Maybe it was the effort of the bus journey and sensory overload of being back in a department store, but I just decided: Ben would see me in those trousers and remember why he loved me. And, reflected in his eyes, I'd remember why I was loveable. The stripe down the side was symbolic of the track that we'd get back on.

A few weeks later, Una saw us off at LAX airport, where we were on our way to meet Ben in the UK. We were parting ways there because Una had not mentioned in the interview that 1) she was terrified of flying, and 2) her passport had expired – and I hadn't thought to ask. Just like I hadn't thought to ask Ben if he had any hesitation about childcare. For someone whose career had started in journalism, I did not ask anybody anywhere in my orbit any of the most basic questions. I asked them interesting abstract ones. I think this made for good interviews and less successful life choices.

The tiny baby had her own business class seat – the first sign of the gap between where we'd been and where we were now heading. An economic version of the 'soul lag' William Gibson describes in the novel *Neuromancer*.

We reunited with Ben at the Chiswick rental house in West London, me having excitedly changed into my new Katharine Hepburn trousers on the way. To return to Chiswick is to return to tree-lined streets and bad feelings. Nobody is at ease with themselves where they grew up – it's where you feel least in touch with your core and you wobble from room to room holding onto furniture like a baby learning to walk. Ben kissed me but quickly appeared ill at ease, an inscrutable look on his face. Though we'd only just got there, he suggested we push the buggy to my mother's.

We were halfway there, when he asked, 'Are those new?'

'Yes,' I beamed. 'I got them in the Nordstrom sale.'

He whispered, 'Burn those trousers. They're so terrible. That's not your arse. That's not your arse.'

If he said it one more time, it would be like summoning Candyman, but instead he said, 'Just burn them.'

I would have preferred it if he had summoned Candyman, because at least then I'd have been dead. As it was, I had to keep walking.

The clothes our lovers wear are of great significance. There is a seismic relationship gap from 'you must remove these immediately because I want you' to 'you must keep this garment on while we fuck because it is underlining just how much I desire you' to 'you must remove and burn these because they offend my eyes'. The worst clothes are just crime-scene markings around the corpse of your dead relationship.

The whole marriage had very quickly begun to feel like trousers that didn't suit me. I saw the trousers reflected in a café window as he took over pushing the buggy. When I was pushing, they looked fine. But just as myself, without leaning all of my body weight forwards, without existing purely in service of a baby, he was right: they needed to be removed and if not burned, then never spoken of again – put away, donated.

Perhaps you could donate a marriage to someone who could make better use of it . . . Just leave it in a bag on your doorstep on a Tuesday and have it collected. But I was halfway to my destination. I could not just take my trousers or my marriage off, right there in the sun-dappled suburban street.

But when? We'd just got married and had a baby. When could it end – the sheer and utter heartbreak and humiliation of knowing that you chose wrong? When you cut it down to three words, that fabric feels so light and so easy, though really its weight is sweaty, cloying: *we chose wrong*.

Jemima Kirke and her then husband Mike told us they'd decided we were the coolest couple they knew. This is a big deal from Jemima, who believes it is elegant for women to have red lipstick and slight moustaches. Though I knew she was wrong, that we were not cool, that I felt self-conscious with a slight moustache, that we were on a path to destruction – should we hold together anyway to be admired? Can you be the menorah in the window bringing light to the passer-by if you know you are a fraud?

I kept thinking to myself, I have an old and sickly cat. It would affect my ability to mother if I had to deal with the dissolution of the marriage, followed by the death of the cat. It would have to be the other way round. Because Perry had been with me when I was young and weak, and then when I was pretty young and pretty strong. And then when I was meeting Ben and becoming . . . becoming mesmerised by him and forgetting who I was, let alone what age I'd reached. The cat's death would be worse than a divorce. That's what I felt at the time as I secretly promised: I'll have to keep trying for as long as Perry is still alive.

I remember, still married, missing him as if I'd already seen outside to life past our broken unit. Quietly watching him play his video game *The Last of Us* was almost intimacy, was almost touching. It is a beautiful game. *They* had a happy ending, if you played it right.

I bought so many silky, touchable things. *I* touched them. I started stashing a small amount of cash every week from a joint account, putting it in the bottom of a nappy drawer because I knew he wouldn't look there – and I put away the latex. This was emotional training for divorce: 1) utilisation of a hidden compartment, and 2) packing away, unused, the fabric of seduction. By unspoken agreement, we were done with that. There would be no fabric, natural or man-made, that could bind us back together.

There was one final attempt to connect. I had a research weekend in Paris for a book I was adapting to film. We both worked hard to make the trip happen. It was in the apartment of the bookshop Shakespeare and Company, only open to visiting authors. Maybe it was an attempt to beckon back some power, that we had been gifted this because of my job, not his.

You should get in there, among all those stories of other lives. And it's such a magical place to be, the very invite so alluring, that you tear each other's clothes off. But that's not what happened. We circled each other like satellites. We just couldn't do it.

Of course, people have been overwhelmed by despair in cities of great beauty. It's a particular knife I couldn't name until my daughter was old enough to use the special Lego tool designed to separate two pieces too tightly wedged together. When sex goes wrong – not rape or assault, but consensual sex – not only do you not meet in it, but it also pulls you apart. The babysitter, the overnight fees, the Eurostar fare, the child left alone missing you. For what? For the thing every writer has absolute control over. For that which, as a mother, was completely out of my control: The End.

The next day, when we were home in separate beds, the Bataclan was attacked. The small sorrow of our separation linked, in our memory, to the full, murderous horror. I wonder about the couples there at the concert, who didn't argue the way we did, who might have made long lives together.

In early 2016, the feeling was never far from me that we were going to have to call time. And though I was very worried, I had an even bigger nagging feeling. I had become fixated on the health of George Michael. This could be Cassandra-style foresight, or it could, given his lifestyle, just be pragmatism. Either way, I wanted George to know how much his music meant to me. I wrote him a letter, but didn't mail it and David Bowie died, instead.

Ben and I are both autodidacts who dropped out of high school. The last time I sat a school exam, it was a history GCSE in which I was required to write an essay about the golden years of the Weimar Republic. Unprepared, I panicked and thought it would be OK to write an essay about 'Golden Years by David Bowie' instead. I tell you, because it's one of his favourite stories about me – something he enjoyed hearing when he felt tender.

We had just got back from watching Ben not win a Golden Globe for *Bloodline* when the news came through. I don't know if it's more unsettling to get bad news naked or in black tie, but we listened to his songs late into the night and the marriage hung on. When it emerged that

Bowie had known he only had a year to live and had thrown himself into completing an album, I thought about knowing you're going to die and knowing that the thing you must do is work. I thought about how to leave a legacy inside the marriage in the likelihood it would soon be gone.

I almost ended it late one night, during a tense disagreement about parenting. This was really it – we were breaking up there and then – when someone with a flashlight approached our home. Ben grabbed a long kitchen knife and ran outside.

'Get the fuck off my property! I will fucking gut you!'

And we held each other and trembled, and were so glad not to have broken up, to be held by spit and glue, that it took until the next day to realise.

'Ben, it wasn't the meal delivery service being dropped off, was it?'

'Oh!' he said. 'Oh dear. You should probably call and apologise.'

After another fight, my daughter and I ended up at a friend's beach cottage for two weeks, our longest break from each other. While we were there, Prince died. These musicians we loved so much, who had been our sacred texts on dark nights of the soul, were dying, while we were dying on the inside.

I had a very different relationship with loneliness when I was younger. I lived my life in walking cities (London and then New York), where my mood could be best summarised as 'music heard through headphones' and loneliness was something I let melt under my tongue like a sucking sweet, combating the cabin air pressure of my head.

With many, many swear words in his arsenal, 'how *lonely*' is Ben's most frequent insult. It could apply to everything from a denim jacket sold with pre-applied patches, to a misguided nickname, to a poorly considered For Your Consideration campaign. Loneliness is the greatest damnation he can assign to a person, place or thing.

I remember walking down to the beach, looking out at the Pacific, thinking, I don't want to end up lonely, but if we don't end this marriage that needs to end, the icons of our youth will keep dying before their time. (It is the artist's way to believe that not only are they useless pieces of shit, but also that they control the oceans. Ben understood that.)

Leonard Cohen's passing actually came as a moment of respite. Of all the celebrity deaths of 2016, it is the only one that can be described as a good death. Leonard, one senses, simply meditated himself off this plane, a peaceful protest against the state of the nation.

After we finished the film, Ben moved out to where I first knew him – the guest house at the top of Laurel Canyon. He would come to put our daughter to bed a few times a week and we'd orbit each other in silence, two waning moons. To hear him apologise when he walked in on me changing was crushing. How do you look at someone whose clothes you once wanted to tear off, when there is laundry to be done?

How are you going to get divorced, especially with a child involved? Are you going to say, 'I find I am not connecting with this jazz drummer's emotional journey?' Or do you eject the marriage, spit on it and throw it out of the window? Like most couples who were once deeply in love, we did both.

One afternoon, after we'd separated, he called me before he had dental surgery.

'You get us divorced now.'

'Now?'

'Now, or I'll do it, but I'm trying to be a gentleman. Do it by tonight or I'll do it myself.'

Like, after all that, divorce was a pavement drawing Bert could hastily sketch for Mary Poppins to jump into – now everyone's divorced! Isn't it magical and you just have to close your eyes and *leap*!

On Christmas day, I made blinis with caviar and he thanked me, politely. We were still not sure how to hug, so we didn't. Our kid ripped from present to present as if she were pollinating them, and Ben gingerly gave me a maritime-themed cushion with a removable octopus. A completely random gift that said: I have no idea what we are to each other any more.

He was in the garden smoking when I read about George Michael. When I told him, he put me on his knee, and I leaned on his chest and we both cried. I don't know if he was just relieved to see me not crying over our divorce.

'I said it would be him.'

He held me tighter: 'You did. You did say it.'

'It just hurts so much,' I gulped, 'that someone who comforted so many people didn't feel good about himself.'

Ben answered, 'That's why *we* do what we do.'

Later, I remembered the way George's songs swing back and forth from a desperate yearning for closeness to a primal need for freedom. When we finished crying, we danced to his greatest hits, all three of us, and it was a beautiful Christmas.

The next day I told Una. A deeply empathetic woman, she just looked at me and asked, 'Which one was he?'

'George. George Michael. English. Greek. Wham? He wrote some of the most perfect songs in the history of pop. He had a big, big heart.'

She thought a long time before her eyes filled with recognition: 'Toilet Man?'

It felt like a sense memory from couples therapy: you could flood the world with beauty, yet only be remembered for your perceived transgressions.

Carrie Fisher died before the year was done. Soon, Ben and I would descend into six months of froideur as the financials got hammered out. The last time he was tender with me, he called to tell me about Debbie Reynolds. All he said was, 'Mumma's gone now.' I understood right away. I also understood he wanted to be the one to tell me, aware how entwined I am with the family he took me from and to whom he was returning me.

The next time he visited, he was wearing new black wax jeans I couldn't make sense of – and the fact I couldn't make sense of them felt insurmountable (*sometimes the clothes do not make the man*). Around the time Tom Petty died twice in one day was the lowest. My kid and I left the East LA family home for a rental in North London while we tried to find our feet.

I wanted the explosions of the 'Freedom! '90' video. I wanted them when I signed over the house to him (Freedom! BAM!), when I signed the divorce papers (BAM!).

I wanted to re-enter our flat after a Tesco shop to find a flaming jacket with 'Rocker's Revenge', Naomi Campbell observing me from inside a sweater, Christy Turlington crawling on her hands and knees. An unnamed male model doing pull-ups – unnamed because the man doesn't really matter, the man has never really mattered – he's just a reason to buy clothes and plane tickets.

Of course, right when we first split, I thought I would die. I thought I would melt. I thought *I* would end. I have never known unhappiness like it in my life.

And then . . .

I didn't die.

Looking at myself in shock and creeping fascination: I didn't die? But I melted enough, I think, to be malleable for what came in the next years.

We didn't touch again. Not until after filing for divorce – then we were free. That was weird. Then, after a whole pre-divorce year of not touching, we touched *all the time.*

Yes, in the weeks after we filed, we made out and had sex a lot. Other divorcing couples I knew did that. I suppose the body knows it has one last chance to make a baby. He whispers in my ear: 'You're the only one I ever married.'

I pant: 'I know.'

'I'm going to have to come by and fuck you sometimes,' he continues.

'Of course,' I breathed. 'Of course.'

But that's not at all what happened.

Once, after we'd split and got past the acrimoniousness of divorce, we found ourselves watching the 1930s version of *Cat People* together. Val Lewton's strange masterpiece is about a troubled young woman who goes mad believing that when she is sexually aroused, she becomes a killer panther. It's a film I've always loved.

'I wish you'd made me watch this at the start,' sighed Ben. 'I'd have understood you better.'

Does he think that I'm frigid? Does he think that I'm delusional? Does he just think I'm not made for domesticity?

But most importantly: who will I talk about old movies with? There was my husband and my parents and the first is gone and the others will be. You are scared and sad, you don't know how to talk to each other about your hurt, but you *can* watch films together. That's something. It doesn't feel like nothing.

The foam symbols baristas leave in lattes took on great significance to me, both as a new divorcee and a late-in-life pothead. This beautiful young person behind the counter wishes me so much love that they want me to drink a heart? Gratitude and stoned-ness are interchangeable, or one has caused the other to blossom. Like so much good that's come my way, I couldn't have done it without living in LA.

Ben admitted that part of falling for me was that I didn't smoke, drink or take drugs, and that made me a preferable mother than some others he'd been eyeing. In 2017, two things happened in synchronicity: the marriage dissolved as Prop 64 was introduced. Soon, I was separated and cannabis had become legal. LA immediately set about doing its thing: utilising beauty for the purposes of capitalism, the sleek weed-tasting salons with their chrome counters no more insidious than MGM altering Rita Hayworth's hairline. Out with the connotations of depressed/studenty, under the carpet: the history of incarcerating African Americans for minor drug offences. LA instantly redesigned cannabis as aspirational.

It *really* worked. More than any man I know, I'll do anything in the face of beauty. I think the three most beautiful things in LA are the palm trees, bending towards water, art deco apartments with built-in vanity tables. And the Beboe vape pen. Exceptional rose gold with delicate tattoos on its body, that copper glint, like the tumbling of Rita Hayworth's hair in a supper club.

In the first week it became legal, all of the mums I knew thought the same thing: I've dropped her at school, I should try edibles now! But the other mums weren't as inexperienced. I got fucked up.

As I walked to my Pilates session with Audrey – who had been my teacher but become my friend – I started to realise what was happening, as I could barely move one foot in front of the other. It just got worse. When Audrey grasped what was going on, she barely batted an eye. Everyone in LA was stoned. I got more so with every minute, my stirruped limbs dancing through the air as we blasted Bob Dylan 'Isis' Live 1974.

Realising I was as high as the kite from Mary Poppins that represents the parent who missed childhood fun, Audrey insisted on driving me home afterwards. Trying to keep me in the good place, she encouraged me to bellow the theme to *Cheers*.

Making your way in the world today
Takes everything you've got!

I think of all the wonderful female writers acclaimed for their late in life success. And how no one is going to applaud you for becoming a late-in-life pot smoker. If I'd vaped weed before now, I might not have been so hung up on the things I cared about in my marriage and we might have made it. But if I had vaped weed, I wouldn't have been the straight-edge girl he prized.

Coincidentally, the day I started vaping was the evening a city worker accidentally left the gate to the reservoir unlocked. Until they realised what they'd done, the water was accessible for the first time since we'd lived there. I walked all the way round its perimeter, ecstatic, the moon engorged. It hit me that my marriage was something I'd crept into because he'd accidentally left his own security fence open. It was a mistake. It was so damn beautiful. It was time to go back.

❋

As my daughter and I explored North London together, I found that every other street had an amazing view. I played Petty, George, Bowie, Prince, Leonard to her. She only needs to hear a tune once to sing it perfectly. My mum sang with her and it was soothing to watch. I was glad to be re-entangled with my parents in a new way, all of us at different life stages.

Every day at school, my daughter's class of five-year-olds began with them singing 'If You Want to Sing Out, Sing Out' by Cat Stevens. She'd come to love it so much and become so accustomed to our favourite singers being dead that she summoned the courage to ask: 'Is Cat Stevens . . . is he dead?'

'No,' I said. 'Cat Stevens is alive.'

I didn't say, 'He has transfigured. He is at once what he was and something new, but still the same soul.'

I just put her tiny hand in mine and said, 'He's still alive.'

Before bed, I showed her the *Untogether* wrap gift that Jemima Kirke had given me: how she'd taken my wedding dress and personally dyed it dusky pink, so it could be worn to parties.

One day, after dropping my daughter at school, I found myself wandering Highgate. Eventually, I was at the cemetery, admiring the flowers and books at the graves of Karl Marx and Douglas Adams. The thing I found most painful about divorce is that there was no marked spot at which to leave offerings.

The guard said visitors could only go to George Michael's grave if they knew him. I felt like I could pull that off. I have chutzpah. The first time we met, I walked up to Ben and told him I had been looking for him. But it's hard to flex chutzpah when you're exhausted. Waking, feeding, dressing, brushing, getting a kid out of the door to catch the bus in the rain every single day. Returned to a walking city, the music in my ears was my salvation.

'Did you know him?' the guard asked.

'No. I didn't know him. I just loved him.'

> I don't belong to you
> And you don't belong to me.

It is very sad that a big city feminist found it so hard to get along with a hyper macho Australian of a certain age. It's sad, but it's also just the plot of *Crocodile Dundee*. Life is melancholy and it's ridiculous and it's that combination that, like a brilliant pop composition, is worth replaying. Songs are the place to leave offerings for everything you lost and everything that stayed, and they're the flowers, too.

Part Six

When I think about the walls I consciously put up by choosing celibacy, I remember this: once, I was a princess in a tower, and I loved it.

OK, I was a part-time princess, locked part-time in a full-time tower.

It was 2010, the year before I met Ben, and I had an antique desk and an ancient laptop in front of me. From my window I looked out over a rolling Tuscan valley in Italy. I had no air conditioning, but the stone walls were cool and dark – fifteenth-century air con that still worked. Tilling the garden in a large-brimmed straw hat and blue sundress smudged with soil was a strikingly beautiful redhead in her sixties: Susa, whose late husband had bequeathed her this fifteenth-century estate. Determined to keep the working farm running, up close she looked like recent photos of Jacqueline Bissett, but from this distance she embodied an aura of freedom and independence. She was the ideal hostess for a non-conventional set-up.

I'd ended up writing in her tower wing via a film producer, who I was then seeing. I was also working with him and he'd had me hired to rewrite the script of a film he was to produce.

'Finally!' I joked when my agent called me from LA. 'Finally, I slept with the right person.'

My agent laughed nervously.

He'd pull the rope to ring a courtyard bell, signalling that I was to come to the library and start working out our draft for the day. Then, I'd be sent to my tower to put the ideas to paper. When that was done, we had lunch, then we'd retire to our separate rooms and he'd climb the stairs to my room for sex. Afterwards, we'd siesta in separate rooms. Then he'd ring the courtyard bell again and we went back to work, me again facing out onto the valley. After supper, we wouldn't see each other until the next day. Sex was not for night.

'Night,' he said, 'is for sleeping,' which I found very charming. I loved the whole arrangement.

Susa, the woman in the garden, the mistress of the house, became one of my mentors. I wrote much of my last memoir in that tower. She had a huge life. Her husband saw her waiting for her connecting flight at an airport and told her to come away with him. She went!

She has an interesting way of expressing deep emotion that gives way to tart common sense, like rhubarb with ice cream. After she read my memoir about mental health, she said, 'It's beautiful. And it's done. Let it go now. Let go of the balloon string.'

You have talked about it – you don't need to talk about it any more. Which is not the British 'stiff upper lip' but rather a compliment: you've said it as well as you can, you can shut up now. It's not feelings-oriented but quality control.

I loved her. In those years, I was used to getting a glow from how powerful men saw something in me. This boyfriend, the one before, the one before that. Nothing kids said about me at school could hold weight – no whispered disparagement from the first love could stick. As long as these men wanted to be inside me, I was not an outsider any more.

But Susa's gaze tickled me more than any man I'd taken up with. I could see from the way she'd chosen me that not only was I of value now, but also that I had decades ahead to grow in power, as she clearly had. This independent, courageous beauty of hers was as intoxicating as the poppy fields that surrounded us. One day I'd be ripe and could smoke myself. That's how I'd ultimately pass away. A *peaceful* version of Tom Petty feeding Alice to herself.

As all kids do, CJ likes to play in my jewellery box. She slips pieces onto herself and also enjoys styling them on me. After letting her load me up with Grandma Emma's Indian jade bangle and Great-Aunt Lil's charm bracelet, I superstitiously decline to let her push my wedding band back up my ring finger. If you wear a ring on your ring finger, you don't get married again, right?

But would that be so bad? Of course not. It's only that you want to leave open the possibility that you could marry in old age, like Gloria Steinem. Yes. This is a soothing thought. It's only that . . . marrying at the age Gloria Steinem did might be as futile a fantasy as dyeing your hair the auburn shade of Sophia Loren's. You are you. You are not her.

In Tuscany, the producer once took a ring from his finger and placed it on mine as a gift. He'd had it made in a store in Venice, California. In a move that made less and less sense as time passed, I deliberately left it behind in our room when I returned to London ahead of him, to imply that I didn't care about it or him. When I did care.

By the time I landed, I got the message in which he broke up with me. The shop he bought it from folded, but I'm still on their mailing list. They update shoppers about their family now. They don't know me and I don't know them, and I wonder what became of that ring he gave me that I left on the bedside table.

I was totally fine with it not working out with the producer, the grand Guignol of his decision hilarious to me. But the truth is, I really wasn't fine and it wasn't hilarious – it was just sad. And exhausting. This. Again. But quicker.

At that time, he was in a bad patch of his career and I was present for it, which can feel like being party to it or maybe even being the cause. If you cease hanging out with that person, at least one of you will end up in the right place. And starting again with someone new is also understandable – you know you will be happy, even if it's just for a while. I just didn't like him choosing someone else for the actual thing of a conventional domestic relationship, even though I'd had such an incredible time not being in one.

I said I'd write a romcom about it and he said great, he'd produce it, and then I wrote it. I made both of us sound awful, *which we were*, and I didn't hear back from him. When I eventually did, he was quietly apoplectic, the worst kind of apoplexy: one that had been run through a therapist.

Despite breaking up the brief romance, the producer was actually very supportive when my first memoir came out. He told me he wouldn't be able to make it to my book launch as he was editing his grand period piece, then when he showed up, I was delighted.

'I did that on purpose,' he said. 'I told you I wouldn't be able to come, so you'd be extra pleased to see me.'

He made me laugh a great deal – a combination, much like Ben, of laughing both *with* and *at*.

I always idolised creative couples but didn't take into account that they tend not to last: Paul Simon and Carrie Fisher, Carly Simon and James Taylor. Steve Martin and Eve Babitz. My personal favourite: Albert Brooks and Linda Ronstadt.

Over the time I worked there in Italy with the producer ex, he completely rewired my work ethic and even now we don't speak and maybe he even considers me an adversary, I got to keep that. The ghost chorus of exes, though they possibly despise you, make your life more expansive. Disgust is passed from one to another in a relay race, as each moves on as quickly as possible to the next person to prove that it was *you* that made them feel bad. Maybe hatred presses against the edges of your life and puffs it out, and that's why everything has come to feel so possible now.

I think many of my romantic choices and sexual longings *have* been good for my career; but not in the way you'd think. At least not *just* the way you think. Would I have been hired to work with the producer if I hadn't been involved with him? Unclear. I deserved to be, but likely I would not have been on the producer's radar.

These men who have great skill and accomplishment in their field have left me with so much to contemplate once they are gone. There are not only practical rules I've absorbed from them about how to sit down and work, but also streets in my own heart I didn't know were there until my lovers illuminated them for me. They showed me shortcuts. Said, 'Have you ever tried getting there this way?'

❋

I banged out the original draft of *Untogether* when Ben and I first met. I was writing on the page what I hoped our love story would become, whereas in the real world, I was less honest, saying silly things like, 'I don't want to be your girlfriend. I don't want to be anyone's girlfriend.' I always say this and I never mean it.

'You said,' adds Ben, when we recall the beginning, '"I'm not like other girls." Ridiculous!'

'And you said jaaaaaaam.'

After our first night together, we had gone in at daybreak to the Laurel Canyon General Store, where he was cruising up the aisles, picking up item after item to purchase – this is when he had no money – when he said what he was really on the hunt for was jam. Only his Melbourne mangling stretched the word out so long, I ought to have known then we'd end up forever entwined.

I wrote the role of Martin in *Untogether* for Ben, to showcase his guileless, joyful side, the half of him that's Iggy Pop just wanting to be your dog.

It felt important to get it filmed before we ended up divorcing. After a decade as a screenwriter, it would be my first film as director. As financing finally fell into place, partly on Ben's participation, I realised I'd have to direct my husband as we were pulling apart.

What kind of person am I that I was able to grit my teeth through that?

A person who had been trying to get a film made since they sold their first screenplay at twenty-five. A person who had worked, since then, constantly in film, only everything had always fallen apart before making it to the screen – I was paying my rent via acres of unfinished architecture. I had to get this film made. Being party to Ben's late career blossoming (after he'd been getting kicked back by Hollywood for over twenty years) was both gratifying and difficult. I could not walk in peace from this marriage in which I'd helped to jump-start his US film career if mine was to be abandoned beside it.

At the start of the marriage, I had been the breadwinner and the radiant success, and once we were at the end, he was the earner and the radiant success.

When I ran into an agent who had tried to court me as a client, he said, 'Do you still write?' And before I could answer, he quickly said, 'You don't need to, I guess. You've got a baby now.'

I had stopped mattering in the marriage. And I'd stopped mattering in the town. It was shattering.

At the end, I thought of my marriage as having been in an elevator with Ben. What I made daily peace with was the possibility that, because of having a wife and baby, he – already sublimely gifted – was perceived by the industry for the first time as domesticated and therefore more reliable. Producers and directors knew that if he didn't answer his emails or texts, they could ask me to corral him, which was frequent. He had been elevated and I had been left trapped somewhere small.

When I was pregnant, I introduced Ben to the producer who had made me a princess in a tower and I watched them circle each other like cats.

'He was wearing eyeliner and nail polish!' Ben noted, tickled.

'I haven't heard of him or seen any of his films, but if you say he's a good actor, I believe you,' was the producer's review.

Soon enough, he watched Ben's film, and cast him in his own. When Ben and I separated, they kept working together, to some acclaim. It was one of the more painful aspects during that bad time – I resented being acknowledged by neither for having set their collaboration in motion.

Men can be tied together by not just sexual history (as I am to both of them), but also by the purity of their work.

'You are an old-fashioned king-maker and courtesan,' said Ben, who thinks I see a slight where I ought to see a compliment. 'Introducing us was a courtesan move. You're one of a dying breed, Fozzy.'

Recently, I finally had the guts to ask Ben whether or not he thought I was wrong to have expected some acknowledgment from both him and the producer.

'Why couldn't you or he ever have thanked me for bringing you together?'

He lit his cigarette.

'I don't think you're wrong from an emotional point of view, Foz. I get it. The counter factual is: what did you hope our acknowledging you would result in?'

I say, 'That's a good question.' And, 'I'll think about it.'

But, watching the smoke curl higher and higher, we both know the answer. Some crumb of power. Some soupçon of a sliver of a wafer of my power back.

I didn't know if it was OK with the producer for me to keep seeing Susa after we ended, but I did – more messy boundaries that I rationalised because he had come to her through his own messy boundaries.

His previous girlfriend had been a classmate of one of the daughters; when they broke up, he kept going back there, and so when he and I broke up, I kept going back there. The logic of someone who just plain wants something. When I went back to Tuscany post-producer and pre-baby, Susa and I would walk a valley to dinners of pizza or truffles. We'd go alone, sometimes, to get *gelato*. She'd drop me at the Prada outlet store, the expression on her un-botoxed face the right combination of amused and judgemental when I'd return with myriad bags. She smiled at my devotion to fantasy, when she was offering this life of feet-in-the-earth glamour.

I'd only taken Ben there once, early in our courtship. He had covered Susa's dining-room table in his Prada outlet purchases, and when I nudged him to pack them back up and take them to his room, he said Susa would not care.

But she looked at him and said, 'I do care. And I'm telling you I care because I feel close enough to you to be truthful.'

And it was astonishing. He could not speak for two days. He asked for hot chocolate but then he did not like how I was making it, so I looked at him and said, 'For fuck's sake, make it yourself!' And he did not speak for two *more* days and then it was time to go. Susa presided over all of it, offering direction and off-stage prompts.

Susa has always said the right things.

After the producer chose someone else to love, Susa gently told me to listen to 'Cactus Tree' by Joni Mitchell, a song about a woman who proclaims herself busy being free.

When I was pregnant, I told her how bad things were between Ben and I, all the shocks I kept getting, and she wrote a beautiful email saying that I would never regret having my daughter.

The best advice. Always.

When I was trying to decide whether or not to leave my marriage, I told her I just got smaller and smaller. I didn't hate myself – I just wasn't a self any more to feel anything towards. It was affecting my parenting. Feeling like a soul moving in molasses, I was slow to catch my daughter when she ran up the street and to comfort her when she fell.

'You have to go,' Susa said. 'I didn't and then once my husband passed away, I decided I'd get a nice boyfriend. But there was no one. It was too late.'

Not needing a boyfriend, but not having the option removed beyond my control as Susa felt it had been for her, who was a great deal more beautiful, graceful and cultured than I. That talk was what prepped me to accept that it would be better for the relationship to end. I don't think a woman needs a partner to be happy. But I am pro-choice, in all its permutations, and I did not like the idea of the option being taken away.

Some thought I should let the film fall away and focus on splitting, but the shots my cinematographer, Autumn Durald, and I had planned gnawed at me as I slept, when I bathed, when I carried shopping from the grocery store. Maybe because it was my version of an optimistic love story, I believed I would simply not be OK if I didn't film it. And that it would mean something to some people, were it to see the light of day.

On top of the romantic was the pragmatic: it had taken years to find financing and now we had it.

Scott LaStaiti had been a producer on one of the previous films that fell apart – the adaptation of my memoir – and he became producer of *Untogether*, working tirelessly. His duties included finding 1.5 million dollars of financing and reading to CJ when we went to Rite Aid and she waddled over with a dollar book of *Bible Stories for Infants*. Scott is the most capable blond man in the business, alongside Ryan Gosling who, as we've established, can carry oak changing tables up tight stairs.

I called Scott three weeks from shooting, having read a text on Ben's phone that wasn't for me, trying to breathe again as I walked along one of the East LA roads that is not supposed to be walked. Cars honking me, I whispered, 'Scott, tell me to keep going with this film.'

'Do you want me to say that?'

'Yes.'

'Keep going with this film.'

After years of false starts, Scott had finally found the financing from five jovial male investors. At our meeting with these potential producers, we tried to block out the boasts from one of them that he was close personal friends with Steve Bannon. 'Steve is a great guy!'

Securing the financing for my film might be the last time I was objectively considered attractive by men I would never be romantically interested in. It was my belief that these were men to whom my appearance was a factor in whether or not to take a chance on a female director. At that first meeting, I had on a denim jumpsuit Ben bought me years ago. I was early, so I bought blue liquid eyeliner from Sephora to make them think there was something they didn't understand and should trust me with.

On the way back up the Santa Monica promenade to their office, I dodged the mad homeless whom I could not understand and from whom nobody wanted to learn. As I wove through them, I was glad I had on flat Converse and prayed to G-d, via my trainers: 'If you give me the money to make this film, I'll move fast on my feet.'

'We don't know who these guys are,' said my new agent.

Scott agreed – they'd only made straight-to-video B-movies before – and said it was up to me whether to take the risk or not. I took the risk. I guess I might not have if my marriage hadn't just collapsed. When we got married, Ben said we 'were very brave and very stupid'. I took this brave and stupid risk, again.

As I see it, three collective traumas occurred at the same time, which not only led to me removing myself from sex with men, but also to avoid interacting with them completely. There was divorce. There was Trump. And there were the men who produced *Untogether*; it is safe to say we did not enjoy each other.

There was the producer who would tell risqué jokes on set when I was trying to work and when I didn't laugh, he'd nudge me and say, 'You just don't understand my humour yet.' And I said, 'I do – I just don't like it.' The same man insisted his female assistant be present whenever I had to talk to him in his trailer – I assumed in case I lied about being raped.

Throughout the twenty-day shoot, Steve Bannon's pal became increasingly verbally abusive. By the time we came to edit, my young female editor and I had Scott on guard on the other side of the editing suite door because we were so afraid of him.

By the end of my first week filming, we were shooting up at a Mount Washington craftsman house, in the beautiful hills of East LA, when a man I had never met before that day decided that Scott LaStaiti – a most decent man – had disrespected him. I only found this out after (prepping to shoot a delicate scene) I heard the man shrieking, 'I will shut this set down! I will shut this set down!'

Ben, who would not even look in any of the financiers' directions, took a slow drag of his cigarette.

'Take it from me, the actor's actor, that *that* is the cunt's cunt.' Then he turned to me: 'Fozzy? It's going very well.'

Despite it all, I was incredibly grateful Ben was there. Not just because he inspired financing. Not only because he gave a wonderful performance. But because the producers were visibly nervous around him. Marrying a scary man had been a good call.

The night before my first morning on set, I had called my writer–director friend Shana, needing to say out loud what I'd been holding in: that I didn't want to direct this film any more because I didn't want to be on this planet any more. As I sobbed, she gave me the best advice I ever got about film-making:

'Nobody ever gets to direct a film. Women never, ever get to. You're going to make this movie and on the last day, you can have a nervous breakdown and check into a psych ward for ten days, because that's how long it will take for your editor to cut the first assembly.'

It was a twenty-day shoot with a few hours' sleep a night. By the end my face appeared to have melted, like the proverbial cake left in the rain. When I was directing Ben – on the days he shot and only those days – I put on some mascara and it was . . . *how lonely* . . . ? To care how you look in front of someone who you don't want to be with and who does not want to be with you.

Beneath or besides the difficulty of being financed by men I didn't like, there was the presence of wonderful women heading my crew, all on their way up in the industry: my iconic director of photography Autumn Durald (now on *Loki*) unfailingly covering for my inexperience; my costume designer Kammy Lennox (behind the looks on *Pam & Tommy*); my editor Sophie Corra (*Physical*); and Tiffany Anders, currently music supervising the glorious *PEN15*.

A teenage girl interned for us, whose dad, James, was my First Assistant Director. She had overheard me being verbally abused by one of the particularly horrible men on set in a way she was upset by – I was upset by it, too, and I just couldn't see what my options were, beyond taking it and trying to make our days. The option she chose was the sweetest: at the wrap, she handed me a pencil portrait she'd drawn, in which I looked much stronger than I'd ever been.

I have the memory of Jemima's daughter reading to my daughter in bed. And a memory of the full moon; CJ was our third witch, so Lola and I could cast spells in the garden.

There was one other especially significant woman on set. As we entered pre-production, Scott sent me a list of people to interview as my assistant. He'd heard very good things about a girl called Lindsey Raines, who he happened to have seen acting in a play the year before. The utter shame I felt when I asked him, 'Is she very pretty?' And he said, 'Yes. I suppose she is.' And she was. Like a cross between Bambi and Shirley MacLaine, with long auburn hair that CJ instantly wanted to wind her fingers into. I tried to find a way for Ben not to be home when I interviewed her, because that's how insecure I felt by that point.

In my box of precious love letters, one of the most important notes is from Lindsey, who I'd immediately hired as my assistant despite her youth and beauty. She was just too lovely and smart for me to let that pull me under. It was such a terrible time, but she threw out a buoy for me to cling to.

I remember the day she gave me the note. I was so conscious of not going over budget that I had not permitted Ben another take of a scene he felt wasn't there yet. I should have, out of respect for him and out of ease for my job, because it meant he'd shut himself in his trailer, while I'd gone to my own and tried not to have a panic attack while we waited for him. Eventually, Lindsey came to get me.

I was so grateful to have someone gentle to cry in front of, just for a minute. I wiped it away, walked with her to the set and shot the scene. When I came back to get my bag at the end of the day, she'd left me a letter about what a good job she thought I was doing and how proud she was to work with me. Even her handwriting was pretty. Even her cursive looked like what you'd expect the young Shirley MacLaine's to be.

After the film ended, she and my heroic producer Scott LaStaiti got together romantically, and remain that way. So, some good came out of it, or came together from it.

Maybe the financiers I so disliked gave me their money because they thought *I* was a bad person, too. There are several people from the deep past who would posit that about me, I think. Do I believe the deep past? It is so convincing there that I stay away from it. This book is the first time I've touched it in so many years. It's a drug my body isn't built for. The deep past is the concealed trapdoor in the attic of your mind.

I want to be good, like the people I have gathered around me from my thirties onwards. Lindsey, who is decent, thinks that I am. She wrote it down, see? I study that letter the way others track Instagram accounts of ex-boyfriends. A few times a year, I open the box and press the letter to my heart like a posy – from the girl who was so pretty, it scared me.

My director friend Shana had insisted I could have a nervous breakdown when the movie was done. In the end, the gift I got myself when the shoot ended was heart-sore but less expensive than a stay at a psychiatric hospital. I commissioned a pendant on a gold chain by the Angeleno jeweller Andrea Fohrman. On her website, you can calculate what phase the moon was in on the day you were born – was it full, waning, quarter, etc? – and she makes it for you in enamel and gold. Instead of my own, I calculated David Bowie's.

'That's a good-looking pendant,' said Ben one day when we crossed paths in the kitchen.

The enamel side was facing up. I turned it over and held it out to him.

'I had it engraved.'

Still living together, we tried not to engage and he didn't want to come close enough to read it. He really didn't. He took a half-step nearer.

Just be still with me.

He recognised it as a line from 'Cat People' by Bowie and finished the lyric:

Ya wouldn't believe what I've been through.

He allowed himself a half-smile to go with his half-step. 'How very Fozzy.'

Then he walked away. He'd insulted me, sure. But he'd also understood me. He'd cracked – immediately – a code I'd written that no one else had even noticed.

I wondered if this was our rapprochement. It wasn't.

Soon after, CJ and I moved back to London.

Distance makes the heart . . . fester?

When he eventually had to be in a room with me again, his anger at me was electric. I took CJ to visit him on the set of a film he was making in Wales. Divorce in process, burning about the proceeds from his mother's flat, he would not acknowledge me when I delivered her to his room. Unable to shout at me in front of her, he shouted, *venomously*, at the show on TV, which was *Great Canal Journeys*, hosted by husband-and-wife Timothy West and Prunella Scales.

'What the fuck is that? Do you call that a good shot of a canal? Pathetic!'

I tried to make small talk (often, in the last year of the marriage, I'd fall asleep trying to figure out small talk with which to engage my husband when we woke).

'We think my grandma based her accent on Prunella Scales in *Fawlty Towers*.'

Ben made the 'whatever' symbol with his hands, without looking up. Grandma chat is reserved for courting days. *Great Canal Journeys* are for long marriages. I had caused him to segue from 'anger about canal documentaries' to 'fuck you and fuck your grandma' energy.

The wait for my film to come out was interminable. Following our Tribeca Film Festival premiere, we received three good offers of release from reliable studios. The financiers had believed a film with Jamie Dornan would get a huge offer and were aghast, whereas LaStaiti and I thought it was a reasonable amount for an ensemble indie dramedy. Our hearts sank as they said they preferred to self-release the movie. That is the nightmare scenario for me. One assumed a self-released film is only so because no company made an offer to buy it and there they were, turning down three offers. Self-released, I feared the film would barely make it into any cinemas and if it did, it would be there for mere days.

The nightmare scenario is ultimately what happened. The Creative Arts Agency made entreaties on my behalf but to no avail. You work so hard to get the film made, then you battle to keep your cut, that you totally forget to worry about whether or not it will ever come out.

The greatest salve, funnily, as I try not to collapse internally, is seeing other films. I used to go to London's Prince Charles Cinema a lot as a teen, on my own, with gay confidant or unsuitable older men, or, often, with my mum. The joy of running in last minute from the rain after bunking school and finding they're one minute into John Waters' *Hairspray*, and watching it all by myself using £1.99 scraped together in coins! Then there was the 24-hour vampire movie festival, where I saw Kathryn Bigelow's debut, *Near Dark*, for the first time.

So, while I waited to see if my film would ever come out, I took my mum to see the Scorsese documentary about Bob Dylan's *Rolling Thunder Revue*. We were celebrating her ability to move again after months of debilitating hip and back and lung pain that, after myriad tests, was deemed just a facet of old age. It was one of the best cinema experiences I can remember having, joyous as a film and joyous to be watching it with her.

Joan Baez is one of her great heroines, so became one of mine. Joan existed so strongly in her power that she did all she could to help her lover, Bob Dylan, get the recognition she felt he deserved. And it worked because he was a once-in-a-generation genius. But two facts remain: she helped him to be seen. She existed in power before he did. He became a star to eclipse her star, and treated her with contempt. Being both heartbroken and a true artist, she got her signature song from the experience: 'Diamonds and Rust'. The documentary shows them back on the road together, a decade after their bitter romantic break-up.

I think so much about Joan and Bob. How, in the film, she at one point dressed up like him, copying his outfit and kabuki make-up – to make fun of him and to feel closer to him simultaneously. That's how I saw it: like she was getting up in the night to look at his laptop porn as a way to intimacy with someone who has a deep suspicion of intimacy.

Sitting beside her in the dark, I was so elated to see my mum's pain had finally eased. I love her so much my heart could explode. I feel positive and negative echoes from having tried to be a wife, in how I've behaved as a daughter. She is loving, of course. She has made mistakes, of course. But she is 100 per cent the most fun. I get most short-tempered with her and neediest of her time. I see her everywhere, in so many different faces. She is the one. She is my origin story, not just my familial one, but also my superhero or supervillain one, depending on how I feel about myself that day.

We left the film giggling about how Bob Dylan's speaking voice sounds like Jerry Seinfeld and right as we exit, something bizarre happens. My mother trips on a stair that isn't even there and is propelled, with some force, into the marble wall outside the theatre, on which the billboard of future screenings is erected. She tells me she is OK to make it home, but once she gets there, she admits she lied and is in agony. By the next morning, the lung that gives her trouble is making it too painful for her to finish our phone call.

Women have been conditioned to believe that sex appeal and its subtext, fertility, is the be-all and end-all. And if you can't still be fertile, you can at least look sexy. That these are the only viables for an ageing woman: 'She looks great for her age!' Which completely discards the bigger conversation: the viability of the body itself.

I am in my forties and still viable: to lift, to carry, to roughhouse with my kid, to schlep heavy groceries. I can do these alone. I won't be able to manage alone forever, which is where it all becomes circular and fear of not being sexually viable – to catch a partner – is logically instilled in us.

It is one of the myriad reasons that Ben and I remain entwined.

'Until you choose another man,' he says when I apologise for waking him and his girlfriend by calling late at night after our apartment building has been broken into, 'I am still your man.'

Between lockdowns, I took a risk on a late-summer rental in Lyme Regis. It felt a good fit, as CJ is into fossils and I was sifting the past, trusting myself to understand what to treasure and what should be allowed to disintegrate. Because everyone in the UK was booking within the UK, there were no houses left – only something with a games room and far too many bedrooms. I hesitated before remembering I had often regretted money spent on clothes, but never money spent on travel. I convinced my parents to come with us, along with Aoife, of my best mum friends, her husband, Phil, and their three sons. I convinced them it would be a pleasure to have them there as guests and it really was.

Having eased the move back to London by living in a part of it I'd never before set foot in, it was a further exoticism to explore a part of England I'd only known through novels. It is helpful to be a tourist in your own country while concluding a guided walking tour of yourself.

The concept of a British beach is so different from a Californian one. Texturally, you can put a positive spin on it, perceiving the pebbles as witchy runes. But you need sun and God to make the spells come to life, and England doesn't do either of those. So for now, an English beach must be considered spells put in escrow. When she was in her twenties, my mum and her college friends used to take ketamine and go scuba diving in the Caribbean. After motherhood, she liked walking on sandy beaches because it made her bad feet feel better. I figured I could put a portable chair on this pebbly one and though she was barely ambulatory, find a way for her to sit and look out at the sea; though it was grey, not aqua, she's Capricorn and likes earthy tones. Anxiety gnaws at her, but I let her polish her anxieties, sometimes even laying new ones at her feet to work on. I figured, since I couldn't convince her to get help to overcome them, I should let her anxieties engage her the way calorie-counting engaged my grandma in her old age.

The three visiting boys knew they weren't meant to come close to my mum because she's in her eighties and vulnerable. But within moments of meeting, Patrick, the youngest at five, was sitting right next to her, peering into her spectacles through his spectacles. He had the air of a boy in amber – when he was digging through the rocks of the beach, he looked like he was digging through Blitz rubble for DIY toys. My mum deplores other people's children, but she loved Patrick right away so decides the risk is worth it. It made me feel close to her – I, too, will take life risks in the face of great male charisma.

One day, Aoife and Phil took all of the children while I took my mum to the beach so we could be alone. There was always someone there with us – my dad, my sister . . . Alone, I realised we both felt shy. We were looking out at the water, which I watched cross-legged on the pebbles. I reached my arm to hers.

'Sit down!' I said. 'Don't you want to sit down?'

She smiled tightly. 'I can't.'

She was wincing. She took a breath and explained it hurt too much, the moving between positions. That it wracked her body less to stand.

If I abandoned celibacy, I'd be presented or presenting myself as a sexualised older woman. But she is an actual older woman. The week before, she'd tried to get the waiter to come over so she could pay the bill in a restaurant, but to no avail.

'It is hard,' she said, 'being invisible.'

And I know it's true – and she is the most highly visible person in my life apart from Ben, CJ being too much a part of me to count as outside vision, but I still know. If Cat Stevens put his old pre-conversion pictures on a dating app, I'd know what he meant: that he still felt himself to be the same soul. My mother's voice is the same it's always been. Her gaze is. Her eyes are as green. She is young. But not in the ways that make life easier.

Dad was coming soon, to help me help her back up the narrow hill to the rental.

We waited in silence and I could feel there was something she wanted to say. She couldn't quite look at me as she finally asked, 'Have you really decided you don't ever want to have another partner?'

She sounded so sad and scared. My freedom has meant the world to me, but at a time in her life where just getting through the day has felt overwhelming to her, I see I have added to her fears, that she does not enjoy polishing this one, and my heart breaks a little.

My mother is not the only older woman in my life to have reservations about my celibacy.

After our move to London, trying to show CJ that our new life was good, I took her away to Sweden. I took her to Denmark. And I took her with me to Susa's seventieth birthday party in Tuscany.

I was nervous there was something between Susa and I now – in that, in walking away from men, she thought I was walking away from a part of myself. That I was lost entirely to mothering, and that is not what artists do.

I felt sad that I could no longer be the girl she'd first fallen for. I was hurt. I thought I was doing what Joni Mitchell said in 'Cactus Tree' – that I was busy being free. I said of the ex-boyfriend who had introduced us and had recently both got divorced and had a new child: 'I think it is psychotic to move on so quickly.'

And she leaped to his defence, which she wasn't wrong to do. I was speaking of all men who move on faster than the women they leave behind.

But the funny thing was, even though our friendship had been challenged by my celibacy, I still held up the picture of her, working in the sun with her wide-brimmed hat, as a paragon of how good it could feel to be exactly where I am. I see her in a different way than she feels herself to be. Another woman does the same of me, I'm sure. You can't take back a Joni Mitchell song, once handed over, even if the lyrics are misinterpreted. It gave me something to aspire to.

Where Susa lives is one of CJ's happiest places – with sheep, courtyard kittens, a parade of grandchildren and hot-air balloons that rise at dawn over the valley, why wouldn't it be? CJ was buzzing like a hostess from the moment we arrived and it escalated once the party began.

In a room packed with grown-ups in beautiful dresses and farm-hardy shoes, she spent the whole party (hours and hours) tracking the progress of the birthday cake, which was huge and chocolate and looked like the one she'd seen Bruce Bogtrotter consume, to jubilant applause, in *Matilda*. She was so well behaved, entirely focused on waiting for the cake's arrival, following it like we follow an Uber's arrival at a busy intersection on our phone. She declined all food because she was saving herself for the cake. We tend to think of kids existing either in elation or tantrum, but we consider less how much anxiety small people can hold.

When the cake finally reached the living room, and candles were blown out and the knife entered it – seriously, as the knife was bearing through the cake – CJ somehow sensed it was the wrong density. She was right because it was Sachertorte – a grown-up cake for a grown-up party – not especially sweet, no buttercream inside, just bitter marmalade. And when, hackles raised, she tasted it, she burst into tears. Spitting it onto the plate, she had a small emotional breakdown and had to be carted to bed to sob herself to sleep.

I thought of the only date I went on with a man in the period immediately after we divorced. I wasn't what he expected me to be, but then he got into it and by the end, I was taken by his conversation, which was about octopuses being the closest we have on Earth to alien life forms. His eyes were beautiful – that smoke grey I remember from a Dominican doorman in New York.

We walked together to the Tube station and I thought: I could kiss him! It didn't upset me – it made me smile. I agreed to a second date. He arrived and as soon as he sat down next to me, even in the dark of the cinema trailers, I could see his T-shirt was the wrong fabric – that I would not like the feel of it against me. That it would not fall into the right-shaped heap on the bedroom floor were he to remove it, or maybe worse, that it would retain its shape – be an unchanged witness if I were to sleep with him. I was crushed. So I knew how my daughter felt, at the chocolate cake that was the wrong chocolate cake. The hopes she had held for it, existing far beyond its consumption! I wasn't ready for dating and she wasn't ready for new people either, not even a birthday group of them.

It was the end of the party for me. But I wasn't angry because I didn't think it was a case of her being spoiled (like all kids, she can be, but that wasn't it). I understood, right away, that she had sabotaged herself by setting her heart so intently on one thing. Anything can be talismanic. But if you choose just one thing (one cake, or dress, or career, one film to make or one man) and it isn't ultimately as you expected it to be, it can throw you.

This runs counter to how we're raised. The British education system trains us to narrow our focus as soon as we can: to have chosen only three A-level subjects by sixteen, not to mention the one thing we'll specialise in at university. I think it's why I opted out of higher education completely. All you have to do is read children's books to know: to be determined, to be relentless, is to be every heroine of classic literature aimed at girls, from Jo March to Alice.

As my daughter hiccupped herself into a tear-stained slumber, I thought of all the times I've pinned my hopes and expectations on a *thing* – boots, a new red lipstick, a haircut, a new lover – and how they've never filled the fantasy of what I needed them to be, and I've genuinely felt crushed each time. There is no new red lipstick to be invented – all the reds that exist already exist. And yet we still make it our quest: find that magical one that will flatter our complexion and unlock the true potential of our face. I thought about how hard I pursued almost every guy I landed and how weeks after getting them, I knew I'd made a mistake. Splayed like a starfish in her unicorn jammies, I nudged my kid to her side of the bed and remembered climbing into bed with a man I'd worked tirelessly to woo and, as he kissed me, feeling like I'd chosen incorrectly in an identity line-up.

And I just kept going and going, a trail of destruction behind me: in love, in work, in my bank balance. I never stopped to wonder if maybe I didn't need anything at all. That nothing could make my life all that much better.

And when you accept that, the great thing is: nothing can make your life all that much worse. Real life, honestly lived, starts to shimmer with beauty. Real life has the tones to flatter your complexion.

It took me decades to reach this understanding. One of my first memories is of asking my dad to get me a sweatshirt with polka dots for my birthday and then crying because the dots weren't the size I'd meant. It sounds depressing, but it's not. To develop diminished expectations in all areas of my life finally has been a huge gift. It isn't that you should accept a sweatshirt with the wrong size polka dots. It's that the right size polka dots don't exist.

I have to hand it to my kid: from afar, the Sachertorte looked like Bruce Bogtrotter's cake. I mean, from afar I look like Winona Ryder. To live a truly adult life, one in which we feel incarnated rather than as if we are constantly reincarnating, we have to grapple with what things are in actuality, in texture, in scent, in mottled detail. If we can understand that Lauren Hutton is Lauren Hutton *because*, not in spite, of the gap between her teeth, why can't we extend the same flexibility to ourselves?

I don't think diminished expectations applies to love, not in the way you might imagine: I would never advocate for settling. I'd say it's better to be alone, it's certainly no lonelier to be alone (than to settle for less). I got divorced, left behind a decade in sunny California and came back to London to start again. Want to know one of the very first things I realised? No Beverly Hills flower shop has anything as good as a bunch of roses from Marks & Spencer. You know why flowers are better and cheaper here? Because there's a lot more rain.

What can you live with if things don't go the way you thought they were supposed to? I can live with a small place so long as it has a big view. My heart, here, in a two-bed attic flat, feels the same as when I was married and had a big place with a big view. I need a cat. I don't have my favourite cat, my soul cat, who went missing and was found six weeks later, dead in a drain. That wasn't at all how that was supposed to go. But I have a sweet cat.

Your life, most likely, isn't going to be as you thought and yearned for as a kid: to be perfect, to be like others. It won't always be worse, but it may just be different. You're a grown-up. Savour an unexpected flavour. CJ was too little to overcome her cake rage in time to see the sun set and the hot-air balloons take off above the valley, too small to see that beside and beyond the disappointment can lie elevation.

Part Seven

I realise 'separation' is a tragi-comic word to use about two boundary-less people who treat the rules of divorce as mere serving suggestions.

'Wife?' Ben shouts in supermarkets.

'I'm not your wife?'

'Yeah, yeah, wife, ex-wife, *whatever.*' He says it like I'm a woke activist insisting on a newly invented pronoun.

Sometimes, as he has since we first got married, he calls out, 'Wife attack?'

It always conjures *Attack of the 50 Foot Woman*, both attractive and monstrous. He is a ridiculous human being, as am I. There is tenderness to our perception of each other as absurd. And yet, he remains in my sexual memory for a few years after the 'separation'. That doesn't trouble me and I don't beat myself up about it: it simply feels akin to the grocery shop I do from memory every week for CJ, who will only eat the same seven things, over and over, like a melody.

There was that amorphous period when . . . it's not that we might have slept together – that simply was not an option for me. To break my celibacy by having sex with my ex-husband would have been like casting a spell during an eclipse. It would have bounced back on me. But, when he came to London, we went to see a screening of *Black Narcissus* together – a film about independent women with rich inner lives, still going mad from sexual repression! – and he watched the second half lying with his head in my lap. He didn't ask permission and I didn't move him. I was glad he was there.

The constant touching and hugging and deep intimacy and the late nights when he sent me photos of myself at the height of my physical beauty (which, somewhat painfully, we both accept was not my teens, twenties or even early thirties, but five years ago – so near and yet so far) . . . What was it for?

Despite our intimacy, there are definitely things I can't tell him about. If CJ has to go to hospital because of an excessively high fever, or if there's a bully in school, I tell him. But I never mention the primary carer's gossamer shocks: the horror of having shouted at our daughter for making us late for the school bus because she was absorbed in making something beautiful (painstakingly cutting out a string of paper dolls instead of getting dressed). She was confused at the level of my anger and started to sob. I was so ashamed of myself, I snapped: 'And there's fucking Weetabix in your hair!' Like a bulimic attempt to push down bad food with more bad food, terrible feeling on terrible feeling.

Within a minute I whispered, 'I'm sorry. I'm so sorry. I wish I hadn't shouted.'

Though I know it's not the worst thing I've ever done, it felt to me like it was. Philip Roth wrote his short story about a child who tells a rabbi: 'You shouldn't hit people about God.' And it was similarly unforgiveable to me that I chided my daughter about beauty. Paper dolls! I kind of wanted to die. But you can't kind of want to die if you're a single parent. You aren't allowed.

I've lived long enough to assign different tears to different places. I recognised the tears that came on and off all that morning as the same kind of tears that came when I finally saw the Chris Ofili elephant-dung Virgin Mary that had once caused such outrage when it was first displayed in America. Standing alone before it at the Tate, I was overcome. I cried for the painting's loveliness and the wilful misunderstanding around it.

Asceticism has made me an infinitely more sensual being. Abstaining for religious reasons feels an apt comparison, because now I feel religious not all day, every day (there are also itemised bills to pay and stinky rubbish to

Often, Ben will perseverate over a song lyric. When the Jay-Z and Kanye West album *Watch the Throne* came out, he found himself saying the line 'Murder to Excellence', over and over again. The fact it was trapped in his head seemed to be making Ben feel crazy and thus act crazier. I got the words printed for him on a T-shirt, so that they might be on the exterior rather than submerged where he had to fight with them. It is, perhaps, a positive equivalent to the way racists had always felt the things they felt but known never to say them out loud in public, until Trump told them they could.

Other times, he will be so bothered by a lyric, he has to act it out. 'What's that jacket – Margiela?' rapped Kanye, so Ben then had to purchase an expensive Margiela jacket so he could FaceTime me, point to it and say, 'What's that jacket?' over and over until I clicked what came next and said, 'Margiela?' It was like in the Elvis Presley movies where, if he sung the words 'sucking on a lollipop', they'd make him hold a giant lollipop.

After our separation, when Ben really started rolling in dough, he fixated on clothes for clothes' sake. He bought himself a pair of Balenciaga sock shoes – truly, one of the more hideous items on the planet – and then asked me for CJ's shoe size so he could buy her some, too.

As I was gently stewing about how we couldn't afford to have a flat in London with a garden, he kept buying us expensive things we didn't want. So I declined to tell him her shoe size and considered the matter closed.

In February 2020, right before the first lockdown, when we went to LA, Una and Johnny accompanied Ben and CJ to the zoo while I worked. Ben texted to say they were running late coming back due to traffic. However, I knew he had stopped at the Balenciaga store, because Una had called me from there in a state. He had not only dragged Una in, but also her husband, and was insisting they each choose a pair of the Balenciaga sock shoes at his expense.

The shoes cost $800. Understandably, Una would much rather have had the cash than two pairs of ugly shoes. But he was pretty much holding them hostage in the store until they agreed to let him buy them.

'Just choose the least disgusting,' I advised her.

When he pulled up at the house, Una emerged from the car, trembling and holding her Balenciaga shoes in front of her. She looked like she might be sick into them.

I was so pissed, I couldn't meet Ben's eyes. He drove away with the beam of a man who knew he had just made everyone's week.

That night, CJ beside me, her Balenciaga sock shoes beside her, I eventually went to sleep, having accepted it was just Ben and that he was trying to be kind. I thought: I wish I had allowed him that when we were together.

That, instead of conveying disappointment at his wild spending, I'd just smiled and said a thank you when he bought me three pairs of silk pyjamas for my birthday when I'd only asked for one, ten rare edition books for our paper anniversary instead of explaining, like an arse-hole, how much more it would have meant to me if he'd chosen one. I wish I hadn't said those things. That I'd allowed him that pleasure.

The next day, he rolled up early to take CJ to the play-ground. I was sitting on a patio bench in my nightgown as he walked up the path.

'Your mother is so beautiful!' he said and started to take a series of photographs as he moved towards me.

He was smiling, really smiling – he didn't hate me any more. Then he leaned in close to me, brushed my hair from my ear, pressed his lips against my skin. My breath caught as he whispered, 'I would love to buy you a pair of Balenciaga sock shoes.'

Something about how your face looks in Californian light, something about the weeks of warm sun on my body, something about not being hated any more, meant I returned home from that trip, for want of a better word, horny. There was obviously no sun to be had in London, but I still had a TV and iTunes. I could summar-ise a strand of fantasy I revelled in as akin to the Twitter's #CatsWhereTheyShouldntBe, which . . . has photographs of cats in places they shouldn't be.

Roy Orbison's voice – because he is essentially an opera singer in pop – is a good example of the erotic pull of #CatsWhereTheyShouldntBe. As is the comedian Bill Hader's broad shoulders – two seasons into *Barry*, I turned to myself and asked, 'Why does such a gifted comedian-writer-director need the upper body of a marine?'

My emotional vigilance both for and against Cats Where They Shouldn't Be became, in the end, a marker that it was perhaps time to prep for the day when I would again have sex.

'Listen,' I warned my sister, shakily, when she Face-Timed as she was feeding her baby one day, 'I can't talk about Bill Hader's shoulders.'

My sister looked at me, alarmed.

'I wasn't going to.'

When I was twenty-one, there was a beautiful Jewish boy I knew vaguely through a friend. He was twenty-six, smart, funny, handsome, well dressed, extraordinary hair, from a wealthy intellectual family. He'd have been right for me, except he could tell, I think, that I was too short, carried too much weight across my arse and soul, and that my family struggled with money. He didn't say that, but it's how I felt about myself. I sensed, furthermore, that my only point of value was my youthful success, having just published my first novel. It was the thing that intrigued him and kept him inviting me to the occasional group gathering, from which I'd attempt to peel him off alone in rich people's kitchens.

I love-bombed him with Carl Reiner and Mel Brooks audio tapes, but he was uninterested – well, he was very interested in the tapes, but not in me. I'd soon move to America, and he'd soon marry a shiksa goddess and have children with her. And that was the end of the perfect Jewish boy who could see all of my imperfections.

Or so I thought, because who knew there would one day be such a thing as social media . . .

So, some decades later, when I was a few years into celibacy and had moved back to London, he found me on Instagram and asked me out to lunch. It was the first opportunity I'd had to dress up since I'd moved back and I did so with vigour. I went for my red velvet 'divorce' skirt, heels and a grey angora sweater, which was how I dressed when he'd first known me, only now I was refined. My manners were improved. With ageing and motherhood, I'd lost a large amount of weight. And I'd had my nose refined as soon as I moved to America at twenty-one by the specialist in ethnic rhinoplasty – the doctor who had done many of the black, Latina and Jewish stars who no one ever calls out for their nose jobs.

I decided I'd break my Trumpian pact with myself and have sex with this boy-turned-man, in a punitive way, to punish him for how disinterested he was twenty years earlier. So I got to the fancy Chinese restaurant too dressed-up, which seemed to amuse and confuse him. He still had all of his amazing hair, but I noted his teeth had slipped with age – so had mine, that's just what happens, but, exposed to my mother's long-term panic about George Clooney and Jeff Bridges' teeth, I'd been on the case with that and wearing Invisalign, which I'd discreetly remove before the food arrived.

He was interested in my years in the USA, very much so, and we had a great time. And there it was – I would break this sex drought by reaching out a slimmer and more manicured hand to the past. Then at the end of lunch, after paying the bill, he said I must meet his girl-friend, whom he claimed I would love.

I'm bewildered to say that this then happened a few more times with different men in London. I'd meet a man through a friend or at an event, he'd ask for my number and if we could get coffee, we'd get said coffee and he'd say I must meet his wife or girlfriend.

Meanwhile my once young, now middle-aged Jewish friend asked me to join his book group and I accepted, still high on the possibility of . . . Doing to another woman what had been done to me? I only knew it felt intoxicating to interact, to play act, to get lunches and swiftly returned texts, even if all of them were appropriate.

At each book club meeting I'd find ways to brush myself against his sweater as I helped to clear the table. The touch and smell of him was the high point of each month. Furthermore, to be in an adult world, talking about books, was enormous for me, when I'd been around no men deliberately for many years by then and relatively few adults without children as the centre point. Just to normalise being around men was a big step. All the homes were beautiful and I knew it could not be held at my top-floor flat – there literally wasn't room. A rising anger engulfed me that I didn't live somewhere where I could invite people. I dwelled on the house I'd left behind. As if it were my child's end-of-year photo, I showed people pictures of it, with its sparkling lights reflected on the water. The more resentment I felt about what I'd left, the more I felt prepared to act out sexually.

It wouldn't be a nice thing to do, but life just wasn't fair, and there we were.

One night, after book club, he and I shared an Uber and he said, 'How are you doing?'

And, without a beat, I said, 'Well, I feel weird being in an enclosed space with you, because I want us to go to bed together.'

And his response was to say the grown-up words of a once beautiful boy who had grown up and had his teeth slip: he *had* thought of me that way after we reconnected, that it had caused him guilt as his girlfriend was wonderful, and he adored her and wanted to do right by her. And – that was actually fine by me. I felt like I'd got my power back, just not in the way I'd expected. Voicing desire out loud and then *not* acting on it was something I'd never tried before.

Not long after, I went to his son's bar mitzvah and met the man's girlfriend, who was a dream, just very fucking cool. The impression she made on me killed any romantic feeling I had for him.

After I met his girlfriend, sometimes I called him back, sometimes I didn't. I was busy with work and none of my responses to him were planned to gain or lose power. I always enjoyed seeing him, we called each other for advice now and then, but I never yearned for him again. It's interesting to understand that if you don't invest in a crush, if you decline to nurture it, it does not bloom.

And so I continued going home each night with celibacy, having had a first flirtation with what might be on the other side.

The first thing to replace Ben in the masturbatory opus I conduct throughout celibacy is the Netflix documentary about the man and his octopus. This shouldn't be so shocking, since hentai (illustrated tentacle porn) has been a mainstay of Japanese erotica for centuries.

Anyway, the man who made the film *My Octopus Teacher* seems like a huge narcissist – and that's catnip to me. Secondly, when you spend a lot of time coming by yourself, the orgasms get so huge you feel yourself changing shape like the octopus protagonist – I pull and push, and new parts open and reveal themselves and suck me in. I also felt it the time Ben and I made the baby. I was the octopus that night and we both looked at each other, confused about what my body had just done, taking a minute before we mentioned it out loud. So being attracted to the octopus in the film is just a form of being attracted to myself. It's Tom Petty making Alice eat a slice of her own sponge-cake form.

The only problem is, I got the denouement of the video wrong. Sometime during the bad years of marriage, near the end, I rewatched the video for 'Don't Come Around

Here No More' and clocked that Petty was not feeding Alice to herself, but handing out slices to the rest of the band. I found that crushing: not only can't she taste herself, but she is empty calories and none of the men practise mindful eating.

After another year in London, with not a single male talking to me apart from the nice man who had come to the cinema in a T-shirt I didn't like, I succumbed to the earlier suggestion by Marc Spitz's girlfriend and joined a dating app. I put up a picture that I love because my much-missed cat was leaning into my back as I worked. This is the most *me* photograph that exists: writing, in a city with a view, wearing a pretty dress that made me feel powerful like Rita Moreno, with a cat leaning into me. Next to my computer you can see the Richard Avedon photo of Capote and the painting of Blur that hangs in the National Portrait Gallery, and a snapshot of my mother as a young woman. You can see the way I use my touchstones to protect myself.

I liked that the dress in the app photo had history because, if I was going to put myself out there as open to love, I wanted, as company, the ones who had loved me most. The boyfriends hadn't stuck. They weren't meant to. But when we were together, they had truly seen me. When they finally looked away, the hardest thing was to be unseen.

A young man in Hackney quickly messaged me. When I read his message, my stomach lurched.

Is that an Apple iBook? How *old* is that photo?

He didn't even see the dress. It hadn't occurred to me, when I selected my picture, how all of my years had flooded together. The beautiful, burnt orange dress was twenty years old and so, I realised, was the picture. In selecting my photo, I had so deeply absorbed the twelve-step maxim – 'Let us be grateful for what has been given to us, what has been taken and what has been left behind' – that I'd inadvertently committed dating app fraud.

I deleted the app. I put aside the dress for charity.

Then I sat in my room, with my hand on my heart – I don't know why I held my hand there so long, except I suppose I was checking my oath to myself. I put on my jeans, my T-shirt, my grey sweatshirt, army green puffa coat, wet-weather boots – this new uniform for taking two buses to collect my child from school. I didn't feel powerful like Rita Moreno.

Soon enough, I lost my humiliation in the rhythm of the day. That's the gift of the age of responsibilities. As I write this, I miss that burnt orange dress. I hope it was picked up. I hope both owner and dress are happy. Maybe it's been given away again. Maybe it's landfill now. It had a great life, as have I. If that was all the love and all the passion I've been allocated, it was *epic*.

And if someone had replied to the app profile with the right words . . .? Well, in my heart of hearts, if someone had come along offering love, could I still fit it in? If someone incredible had wanted to fuck, would I have had space inside me? I was gripped, in my early twenties, by a hole in my soul that I literally tried to fill with sex. In my forties, there is so much going on inside me – more ideas, more stories, more love for my family and for the world around me – that I don't know if I could also fit a man's penis.

It was 2020 and I had held no hand but my child's since 2016. But if there were a hand in mine, would I find it soothing or controlling? How easily one swerves into the other, and a relationship does not have layers you can remove and put back on at will, a cardigan peeled off and tucked into your bag until the weather changes. Or does it, and I just didn't pack the right layers yet?

If my ex-husband were hiding in a jungle lair after being felled as a dictator, and allied forces wanted to flush him out, they should play 'We Built This City' by Starship.

'Get it away!' he used to shriek, as if the song were crawling up his neck, his position behind the driver's wheel rendering him more vulnerable. 'Disgusting! It is *disgusting.*'

Changing the radio station as fast as I could, I'd agree, it is an unfortunate song, and that the video was certainly an unfortunate look. The male vocalist, Mickey Thomas, though bellowing, wears a delicate short-sleeved blouson while performing a stiff-waisted dance, as if he's never until this moment heard of dance. Though his decibels don't drop, he looks worried – not even stressed, which is at least an extreme. Just low-grade anxious.

But it's Grace Slick, the female vocalist, who has always concerned me. Frosted peach lipstick, her shantung jacket both mandarin-collared and shoulder-padded, she does not even attempt the stiff dance – she looks like she's in shock. Her voice is as powerful as when she was the lead singer of counterculture heroes Jefferson Airplane, but now her teased hair entraps the head from which that voice emerges. Grace Slick was once cool – I would say she was the coolest sixties hippy chick there ever was. An unstoppable force, beautiful but *strange*: the militaristic-psychedelic-tarantella synthesis of 'White Rabbit' and the witches' incantation of 'Somebody to Love', indelible because there was no one else like her. Their album *Surrealistic Pillow* is one of my favourites.

Then Jefferson Airplane became Jefferson Starship and, by the eighties, Starship: unrecognisably changed, both softened and hardened – flattened, really – a baking experiment gone terribly awry.

When Trump swept to power, I recognised the gnawing mystery of 'Who *are* these people who support him?' – that feeling of being adrift from half of humanity – from 'Who are the people who love Starship?' But mainly, when the song appears on the late-night VH1 station, I think of his anxious face and her look of shock, and consider it an allegory for the collapse of a marriage. First, and most obvious, there is no sex in the song. The two singers have zero chemistry and, standing in the same frame, they make each other look worse: more confused about what dancing or singing or humanity is. Like most unsalvageable relationships, the journey of Jefferson Airplane to become Jefferson Starship and then Starship takes them from aspirational, sexy, soothing to bloated and phoney. You want to shake them, as you have wanted to shake actual friends, as actual friends have wanted to shake you, and cry: 'Do you know how incredible you were when you started? Do you see what you've let yourself become?'

You may have built this city on rock and roll. But your city sucks.

(I hear a couples counsellor admonish: 'Emma, Ben, I want you to look at each other and try to phrase it in a constructive way.')

I take a deep breath.

'Ben? Your city has no infrastructure.'

He sits up, taking my hand. 'Emmy? Your city doesn't have a grid, so it is extremely confusing for me to navigate.'

I smile tightly. 'The architecture of your city is from a selection of incongruous periods that fail to complement each other.'

But really, I just want to spit, 'Fuck your city. Rock and roll was a moronic thing to build a city on.'

'It doesn't have to be like this,' I think. 'It doesn't have to.'

(Late night in London, I lean in towards the television . . .)

'Have you no memories of where you lived before? If you let yourself be really still, can you remember what existed in this spot before your city went up? What wildlife was native here before it was displaced by shiny buildings? Who were the original guardians of this land? Think hard. It's important.'

Since stopping having sex and kissing and holding hands, I could feel every one of the men who had ever been inside me. I revisited the greatest loves, I could see into the corners of the rooms we were in, my perspective when he entered me from behind, recall very clearly when I was on all fours or when I lay flat on the bed.

I remembered when I used a vibrator and when I didn't. I remembered the sheets and the curtains and the towels afterwards, and the brand of face wash I used at night. I remembered when I had a rash of spots around the side of my mouth and when my breasts were so epic from birth control, I didn't have to wear a bra. I remembered when I lost weight and they looked to me like bananas when I was in doggy style, so I avoided that. I remembered how I'd cup my arms either side of my breasts to disguise the loss of density when Ben was on top of me, and how he looked down and said, without malice – in fact, with real affection – 'I know what you're doing.'

Since no one except my child has held my hand since I filed for divorce at Christmas 2016, I started my sensual memory excavation with thoughts of holding hands.

When I first moved to New York, there was a kid called Kamen, a musician–skater I'd met that night, who stroked my hand for hours at a house party. I remembered how the energy in his touch was so intense, I felt like I would come. That's it. That's the story. I have no idea where he is. Or who he was. No idea whose party that was. I don't remember what he did for rent money. That was New York. There are endless cirrus clouds in motion when I look back on the human beings I met.

There was a boyfriend – the first epic love, the one I travelled to the ants-in-pants hotel for – who could not hold hands with me in public in case anyone saw and knew he loved a white woman. He'd met me in the summer, when I was tanned, and thought I was Latina and been confused about what I really was – which was right, because I was very confused about who I was.

There was the nerdy Jewish actor, who I'd been friends with for a decade until one night it all changed, the way that it can. He was still a nerdy Jew, but that evening, at a dinner with two of his friends, he discreetly held my hand under the cream-and-red wicker table in the garden of his hotel. Then, when he got me alone in the corridor, he asked if he could show me some Rick Moranis clips on YouTube. And then we went up to his room and had some of the best sex ever, right after we had, in fact, watched Rick Moranis clips on YouTube.

Post-coital, I looked at him and marvelled, 'I thought you were meant to be nice?'

'No, people think that, but I'm really not.'

And the good thing was, even though we'd had illicit, filthy sex, because he's a nerdy Jewish guy he totally understood when I called and asked for my missing underwear back, because my grandma bought it for me for my birthday.

Ben – the night we met, maybe fifteen minutes after meeting – held my hand until I excused myself, needing the ladies' room. When I came out of the loo, he was standing, alone, in the middle of the room calling, 'Baby! Baby!' And I didn't know what was happening until I understood he was looking for me. I'd later learn about 'object permanency' – the fear that people who experienced absent parents have of letting you out of their sight.

There was the friend of Ben's who met up with me one of those times we'd split, only this time I was heavily pregnant.

'You're going to live in my guest house and grow big and beautiful,' he said, and he never let go of my hand.

Some men get turned on by saving friends' wives and girlfriends. I was grateful for the offer to live in his guest house, but I didn't particularly want my hand held.

And then, in 2017, when the divorce was filed, but years from passing, I was at a friend's book launch at a boutique hotel, when the owner came up to introduce himself. I'd stayed there once, when I'd tried to leave my husband. My daughter was with me and I kept thinking, as she breathed beside me, what a great place this hotel would be to have an affair. But I'd been very clear with myself: that this marriage would not end with me having an affair. That was not the right way out.

I was wearing an Agnès B dress I'd bought at seventeen, carrying remarkably lightly all of my other lives I'd had in it, when the hotel owner came over to talk. He was very good-looking.

'I've stayed here,' I told him, not mentioning my child or trying to leave my husband. Instead only saying, 'It was great, but there wasn't any decent lighting at night and that felt unsafe for a woman alone.'

He looked at me and took my hand in his. 'I want to show you something.'

What did he want to show me? I wondered, heart pounding, as he led me past my curious friends and outside into the quiet night air.

'Feel better now?'

I saw that rows of fairy lights had been strung up since my stay. He looked at me. There was no one else around. He was still holding my hand. He came closer.

'Now do you feel safe?'

I caught my breath. The old me would have kissed him. The kind of man I attracted would have put his hand between my legs, pushed me against the wall, right there in the alley. What kind of man was this?

'Yes. I feel safe.

He held my gaze. 'Good.'

Then we went back inside, where all of my friends were staring at us. One took me aside and asked what had happened out there, and I said, 'Nothing.'

The man outside his own hotel was perfect for me in every way. Except, he was not available – was, in fact, said my friend, married with children. I'd see him again from time to time when I ate a quick solo meal at a neighbourhood bar. He'd nod politely and I knew I was tired by then from parenting alone – that I wasn't buzzing with the same wildfire of someone wanting to be free. That I wasn't wearing my past lives lightly and there was nothing I was giving off any more for him to respond to.

It was another celibacy delineator: he would have been the next, but he didn't make a move, so he wasn't and then there was no next, and that was that.

One Saturday night in London, my kid had her first sleepover. Far from taking the evening to pursue a date, I used it to book a massage, and then go home and watch an Almodóvar film while my mum watched the same one in another house and we emailed back and forth about which of the reproduction fifties cardigans was our favourite.

In line for the bus, after the massage, night and cold had fallen, and it was nine minutes away. A few builders done for the day chatted together and, at the other end, two teenage girls dressed for a party debated walking instead of waiting, even though they'd have to pass the woods.

They both wore heavy biker boots and had gamine profiles, and I couldn't stop looking at them. They weren't dressed as I had been at their age (form-fitting sheath dress, hobbling in high heels). They were dressed in loose and low-slung boyish trousers, like the waifs to whom my style had been a reaction. They looked wild, one with a septum ring through her nose, the other with hair dyed green at the tips, but they were nervous about the night and the darkness.

I considered offering to walk them to their party, get them safely past the woods. But the truth is, they'd have been making me feel safer, too. Instead, they headed off and I waited in the lamplight until the bus arrived.

Once Ben and I were getting along, we took our kid to the stage show, *Matilda*. He was a couple of girlfriends post-divorce by then, and I was starting to get a sense that there was nothing on my horizon but motherhood and work. Though we travelled to the theatre together, we peeled off, me to get her an ice cream, he to smoke. He arrived just before curtain, still smoking, sweaty from running. When he got close, I saw that his race for the family musical was weighed down by two overflowing bags from a sex shop. As my sex life had shut down, his had expanded, like the monster in *The X-Files* that can slide under doors.

It moves everywhere, his renewed sexual freedom. But I stay very, very still and it doesn't see me in my hiding place.

Around the time of the theatre trip, Ben had started seeing Paula, the young Brazilian girl, and, as promised, cleared all the other available women for her. One night in LA, by the Formica breakfast nook of what was once my kitchen, he said, 'Fozzy? I want you to give her your blessing. She thinks so highly of you.'

He showed me her photograph, which I squinted at: a beautiful olive-skinned girl with long black hair, full lips, wide smile and dazzling white teeth. I'd been struck by her face the first time I'd seen it, and this was not the first time. I looked up at him.

'I know this girl. I've seen her on my Instagram.'

'Yes! She was a fan of your book and then she became interested in me because she was interested in you. She wrote me a DM on Facebook and the rest is . . .'

I stepped back. He looked at me, quizzical.

'Foz? Doesn't that make you feel powerful? That you're the one who brought us together?'

It's interesting which book you write gets picked up in which country. I'd had one published in Japan, another in Denmark, one in Italy and never at the same time.

Certain books have been snapped up by countries that previously rejected my work. It so happens the memoir his girlfriend loved is my only book I've had published in Brazil.

'I don't know, Ben.'

It made me feel peculiar.

'Just meet her! She's a very *nice* person.'

'I think you should just get on with it and see where it goes.'

'Please, Fozzy?'

'No. You do your thing. You don't need me involved.'

'OK. If you change your mind . . .' He let it drift off. 'I hope you change your mind.'

I nodded, walked out of the room and blocked her on my social media.

❀

My friend Indira is the geographically closest person in my very close circle who lockdown separated us from. A classically beautiful woman a few years my senior, her soul has such bounce that it seems to stream through her shiny black hair and laughing eyes which, combined with the elegant lines of her neck and nose, bear as a visual reminder that you can be buoyant and serious at the same time. During the first lockdown, she and her thirteen-year-old daughter surprised me by bringing my daughter a sixth birthday cake – of course handmade, as no shops were open. They set it at our doorstep, then retreated ten steps back to chat. As a birthday treat, CJ petted their dog, since no one had suggested dogs transmit Covid. When they left, CJ ate their carefully decorated cake with her hands. The level of thought and kindness was exacerbated by our isolation.

One night, I texted Indira:

Are you still awake?

Yes.

There's something I need to say 'out loud'. I have to get it off my chest.

Tell me. I'm listening.

Part of Indira's skill as a stage actress is that she always looks like she's listening to the other actor rather than just waiting for her turn to speak.

I am afraid that no one will ever touch me again. I'm not scared about being alone forever. I don't find that bit frightening. The part about not being touched again scares me.

She didn't say I would have touch again, and I loved her for that.

That night, she gave me the gift of accepting I might be right and it was OK to be afraid. She made me understand that morning would come – and I had told somebody, and they had listened. Our messages were a kind of sensual life, too – a different physical exchange from having sex, but not completely different.

Lola Kirke told me I had been on the wrong dating app and that I must try the one her friend had had 'a good time on'. I agreed I would like to have a good time, that was true, just not necessarily with another human being.

I let her sign me up. I connected with I guess what I was meant to connect with algorithmically: a divorced dad in his fifties. He was successful, well dressed, had all of his own hair and teeth. I was furious about having to go and meet him. The night before we met, he'd sent a long letter about how he'd ordered my memoir, read it in one go and all the ways it had moved him. Just because I'd published a memoir didn't mean I wanted him to read it before a first date. I was resentful and upset.

On meeting him in the park, I was not bored or awkward and I accepted he was, on paper, a good match. I agreed to a second date. But the idea of having sex with him made me cry for the entire cab ride home.

'I don't want anyone to touch me. I feel like I would be betraying the moon,' I whispered to Indira down the phone.

Indira took a stage pause.

'It could be that you feel bad about betraying the moon. Or . . . maybe you just don't want to have sex with this particular guy.'

This hadn't crossed my mind as a solid answer – how quickly we can return to the female factory reset: gratitude to a man for being interested in you.

Back home, I figured out how to let him down gently, this man who had bought and read my memoir in one sitting. I didn't have to send it, as he wrote the next day to say he had quite suddenly met someone else, had strong feelings for her and needed to cancel our next date. I felt absolutely furious and cursed my mother for giving me too high self-esteem. And then I accepted that if a woman you met on an app cried about betraying the moon on the way home after your first date, you might subconsciously pick up on that and quite reasonably cast your net elsewhere.

Ben always said that my taste in home décor was old ladyish and that I was emasculating him with my cornflower blue floral sheets. In our marital home, the 1950s animal print curtains were banished to the kitchen, where he spent his not-yet-woken hours making pot after pot of coffee and was thus able to block them out. Them blocking out the sun while he blocked them out of his mind reminded me of the time a spider emerged from a box of Halloween balloon spiders.

So, in my top-floor flat that wasn't *fair* but was mine, I went hog wild, with my final purchase being a dusky pink art deco stair runner. The purchase was arranged by a nice lady, but once the carpet was in, it was her brother who would be coming by to instal it.

Her brother, when he arrived, was very personable, but he was also, unmistakably, just a really good-looking guy. About my age, with sandy hair and calloused fingers, he looked like an all-American golden boy who had been pickled in a North London pub. As he worked, I brought him cups of tea and we stole small glances at each other. I peeked down, from the top of the spiral staircase, at his hands and the ripples of his back.

Ben had once opined, when he considered getting back in gym shape, 'The purpose of a muscular male arse is to show women you can push.'

I found these statements laughable, the epitome of a 1970s Australian male. And yet, it was absolutely the first thing I thought of when I saw the carpet fitter.

I walked up and down the stairs, finding things to reach for so my shirt would ride up above my belly button. To my relief, he peeked. He could have been looking at me because he was appalled and wanted to commit me to memory in case he needed to provide a police sketch. He could have been. But that wasn't how it felt. I wanted to ask him: Do you have a family? A girlfriend? I wanted to ask, in the long hours he laid the carpet: When you're finished, do you want to go to bed with me – spend the afternoon moving together under the stillness of the pink chandelier?

When he left, I was lost in a daydream. As I let myself ruminate on how we might possibly cross paths again, I stepped backwards and directly onto a long nail he'd left upright.

After I'd finished screaming – every time I thought I'd finished, there was more; a bit more scream squeezed out as if rolling the end of a tube of toothpaste – I had to remove the long nail from the sole of my foot. It hurt so much I went into a kind of shock. As so many times before in my life, physical pain was the instrument that let me tap into psychic pain. I didn't get to sleep with the handsome carpet fitter, but his nail let me accept how much hurt I carried deep, deep inside, accidental S&M.

I *wailed*. For wanting to be touched again. For the re-emergence of myself as a sexual entity and no one to share it with. After I finally finished sobbing, I felt emptied out, like I'd laid an old towel on the pristine carpet and given myself an emotional enema. I quickly felt better, made my own cup of tea, stacked a plate with dark chocolate Hobnobs and started to sing:

> If I were a carpenter
> And you were a lady,
> Would you step on the nail I left?
> And have my baby?

That I even had the confidence, as a middle-aged woman, to assume a man might be looking at me because they're attracted to me and not repulsed by me is a reprimand to the teenage years.

Britpop was an essentially sexless movement, bar Pulp. The scene was basically centred around straight men waiting for Damon Albarn to notice them or Paul Weller to show up. 'I'm not the world's most passionate guy . . .' sang The Kinks, the forebears of Britpop. Yeah, of course no man approached me when I returned to London. Overt female sexuality was highly suspect in my youth.

I remember, a hundred years ago, as a seventeen-year-old, being at a music awards ceremony. I'd thrown off wearing ridiculous Liam Gallagher-emulating cagoules that camouflaged my body in favour of tailored dresses that fitted. That night it was an Agent Provocateur leopard print wiggle dress with buttons down the front.

In the bathroom, as I washed my hands, a very drunk woman in skater trousers, a T-shirt, trainers, spectacles and pigtails entered. Recognising her as the girlfriend of my boyfriend's workmate, I smiled at her. In answer, she nodded at my breasts and snorted, 'Well, *those* are fake.'

I exited, trying not to shut down totally. They were real and I was, too.

'You so easily go into shock,' Ben had said when we were trying to make it work.

I look back decades and see it all, this pattern I never would have noticed without him telling me. And again, I ask myself, why I have returned to the source of the shame. And again I answer: because this is how my life panned out. California with its golden sun, its loving sky, it didn't work out there. I am here.

One particular Britpop moment seared into my memory as both painful and comical was when I experienced anti-Semitism at an orgy. It wasn't really an orgy, it was just a lot of girls with boys' haircuts making out with each other in a bed bookended by boys who had removed the top half of their mod suits. A particularly popular girl I knew by sight but had never met paused from snogging a bleached blonde seductress and, reaching across a member of the band Menswear, pointed at me.

'Who is *she*?'

Several girls from school vouched for me. The popular girl continued staring. When she spoke, her voice dripped poison.

'Has anyone ever told you you look exactly like Bette Midler?'

On the periphery of a bed of Gentiles, the insult worked, though I didn't let her see that.

Then you grow up and realise that, although you understood *exactly* what the remark was intended to evoke, not only is Bette Midler fucking awesome, but she is also *beautiful*. That you would be elated to have her late-seventies cabaret body in her mermaid bikini top get-up, her minuscule waist, triangular Jewfro and all-round sick style.

When we made *Untogether*, I accompanied Jamie Dornan to a show by his comedy hero, the late Don Rickles. Jamie is good-looking, obviously he is, but mainly he's just a really funny, very easy to get along with, man from Belfast. When the lights came up after the show and we saw Bette Midler sitting at the end of our aisle, we turned to each other, both dying to meet her.

'What shall we do?'

He nudged me towards her. 'Say something Jewish.'

I pushed him back. 'No, you say something famous.'

But Jamie couldn't think of a single famous thing to say and, anyway, I was the director.

'Miss Midler,' I stammered, 'we just wanted to tell you . . .'

But she interrupted before I could improvise our spiel.

'No thank you,' she said. 'No thank you!' as she backed away.

She wore the same expression of contempt as the girl at the orgy.

In my version of *Fifty Shades of Grey*, instead of an S&M billionaire, it's just CNN's Jake Tapper, looking exhausted by my bullshit. Through the long wait for the 2020 US presidential election results to be certified, Jake's disapproving expression hovers on the periphery of my mind so insistently that it inevitably got transmuted into erotica until his judgement is no longer on Mitch McConnell and the Republican Party, but on me.

Every single thing I got wrong since I directed my first film and became a divorcee (at the same time), he sees it, he judges me on it, and I will be punished – for this I am grateful. I don't think this is what Fox News mean when they describe something as 'a liberal fantasy'.

'My mum loves this grumpy man with glasses,' my seven-year-old announces as our taxi driver looks up, suburban London stumbling alongside us like drunks singing 'Wonderwall' at closing time.

'Oh, right. Jake Tapper.' I smile tightly.

'She *also* loves this one charming man.'

'Which man?' I ask her. I don't know any charming men.

'He has handsome muscles and he does *Newsround* for grown-ups, too.'

'Chris Cuomo. Mum's just been watching too much CNN because of the election.'

I say it in that way parents do when they're pretending they're addressing their kid but are actually explaining themselves to the other adults in the room.

'But maybe,' she offers, 'the charming, handsome man might like you back . . .'

'Chris Cuomo is a jock.'

'What's a jock?'

'He shows his workouts on Instagram.'

I have shown my workouts on Instagram, too. Now, with a kind of elaborate post-coital contempt of which he will never be aware, I must harshly judge Chris Cuomo for displaying a portion of my own worst qualities.

As a single parent, I sometimes go so long without talking to anyone my age I yearn to talk to my primary-school child in adult language.

'The crush on Chris Cuomo was purely contextual, spurred by the panic and fear of an out-of-control electoral season at a time I was so far from my adopted home. I found reassurance in his steady nightly presence. If he was an estate agent, I would be repulsed by him.'

But I don't say that. And I also don't tell her that her grandma – my mother – spoke insistently of Cuomo's father, the late New York Governor Mario Cuomo, back when I was a young woman in Manhattan. She and the other ladies in her Brandeis alumni circle long pinned their hopes for Democratic President on two politicians:

Joe Biden and Mario Cuomo. What if? What if? She and the ladies seemed to sense it would never be possible, and dreamed ever harder into it, those men representing what the world could be if the world were fair. But when I look back on it now, I see she was also dreaming into her time in New York – the alternate narrative arc of her life if she hadn't come to London, met my father and had us.

And now, during the days we wait, Chris Cuomo tries to calm an anxious nation by saying, 'Slow and low – that is the tempo,' over and over in his sonorous Italian–American voice, and I mean . . . It takes me a beat to realise he's quoting the Beastie Boys, that we must be around the same age, that he is also in a period of thinking about his youth.

My daughter yawns. 'Why can't you get me a charming dad with handsome muscles.'

'You love your dad. He's very charming.'

'I do love him, but his tummy is not like the man on the beach.'

Oh! the man on the beach. The man with no top, who she saw jogging in Sydney two Christmases ago and has become a permanent fixture in her brain. His image returns to her in waves, like those he was jogging between.

'You mean a six-pack?'

'Yes, get a boyfriend with one of those.'

'If *I* get a six-pack, instead of getting a boyfriend with a six-pack, will that do?'

'Yeah. I guess.'

I took CJ to stay at a farm in Cornwall, where she and other young guests helped the farmer feed the animals each morning. We had a lovely time but, soon after we got back, the farmer's wife called to warn me she'd been telephoned by fraudsters who'd accessed my bank account. It seemed to be a money laundering scheme: they'd moved large sums from my account into the accounts of people I'd recently paid. The man on the phone told her he was my husband, that I'd accidentally sent her money by mistake, and was too embarrassed to call her myself, so could she please forward the money to his account. She curtly replied, 'Emma Forrest doesn't have a husband,' and hung up.

The other businesses the fraudsters tried their scheme on were also alert to it being amiss. Except for the man who ran the bespoke spiral staircase business. When I sent him an SOS, it was too late. He said my husband had called to tell him the stupid thing I'd done and that he'd dutifully sent him on the money. I tried very hard to stay calm as I replied: 'But you've never spoken to anyone but me, and we've been communicating for five months. Why would you think I have a husband?'

'Well,' he reasoned, 'He said he was your husband and that you're just a bit dippy and he has to cover for you when you make these silly mistakes.' I was apoplectic: with the man, with the staircase, with the fraudsters, with the ghost husband, whose disdain I felt as cold as metal steps against my bare feet.

★

Once you're a parent, your formative films and lyrics can slowly become unpeeled. It's like audibly hearing the final gasps of aged Blu-Tack behind a *Smash Hits* poster:

Molly Ringwald, why did you tenderly swap earrings at the end of *The Breakfast Club* with a man who spent the entire movie running up and down the halls shouting about his damaged childhood and issues with women?

Or: I see your 'True Colors' . . . and *that's* why I don't like you any more.

And Roy Orbison should *not* have driven all night to get to you. He was legally blind. That is really dangerous.

With middle age comes a new understanding of middle period Stevie Nicks. 'Well, maybe, I'm just thinking, that the rooms are all on fire, every time that you walk in the room.' I totally understand that wild passion and always have, but now, in the slowness of pandemic quarantine, I find it slowly dawning on me: your lover sounds very attractive but, like, also, the room is on fire?

At some point in lockdown, with real theatres shuttered, I went to a drive-through cinema with Aoife, one of my best mum friends. We saw *Jaws*, for no other reason than it fitted our parenting schedule. It was absolutely brilliant, though, the shark seeming to leap from the

Amity water across the North London sky. Like everyone in my life, Aoife was keen to know when I'd date again and afterwards, she asked me, of the heroes in *Jaws*, if I'd rather be with the nice Jewish oceanographer or the devoted family man, Sheriff Brody.

The question sinks my heart because, even though it's just a movie, I know neither of those men would want me. They are normal, so they'd see immediately the ways that I am not. That's how it's always gone.

Aoife, whose husband is a lovely man who helped us to carry our Christmas tree and hang our artwork, is nervous a second until I answer:

'Quint.'

She double-checks she has understood correctly.

'Mad sea-shanty man?'

'No, Aoife, because you *think* he's mad. But remember, it turns out he's traumatised from his terrible wartime experience. Traumatised sea-shanty man. Speaking in shanties is a sign of his *trauma*.'

I think about Ben walking up and down the stairs parroting Kanye's 'Murder to excellence, murder to excellence' over and over until I made him the T-shirt that said 'Murder to Excellence' so he'd stop saying 'Murder to excellence.'

Before we got married, the rabbi had us do five counselling sessions with him to make sure we'd prepped for our new rôles. In two different sessions, Ben wouldn't speak because he was so upset with me. Going through with the wedding because the invitations had already been sent was the same as the *Jaws* mayor telling the media: 'Amity, as you know, means "friendship"!' My romantic inclinations are and always have been the nails on the blackboard that silence the community meeting room.

So confronted do I feel by my attraction to Quint that I ask some American girlfriends whether or not my ever-flourishing crush on CNN's Jake Tapper is also problematic and I just hadn't realised. Should I redirect to masturbating about the Netflix octopus only? My friends confirmed that Jake Tapper is objectively attractive. 'He's smart, talented, funny, handsome,' texts one. And I repeat this several times to myself until it sounds like Trump's infamous 'Person. Woman. Man. Camera. TV' memory boast.

That night, I make peace with the fact that, though I am not sleeping with strange men, it is strange men to whom I remain exclusively drawn. Let's be thankful for Jake Tapper. Let's just stick with watching nightly hours of CNN anchors. Celibacy was a good choice.

By the second November lockdown in 2020, my body felt like a secret swimming cove, restorative and private, even to me. It had to work so I could look after my daughter. So I could carry her into her own bed when she fell asleep in mine – the loveliest feeling in the world.

Eventually, she said she didn't want to be cuddled to sleep any more but that she'd now prefer we pretended we were emperor penguins – we couldn't wrap ourselves around each other, so instead we must simply lie very close together, to protect each other from the cold.

Her endless refrain is 'Leave me alone Stay here' until it sounds like a one-word album title containing boundless energetic power, like *LoveSexy* or *BloodSugarSexMagik*.

I miss my friend Shana, the one CJ thought we couldn't be friends with because our flat was too small. Shana would get high with me and know where to source the best munchies. I could show her my view and, even as an Angeleno, she would be impressed by it. I don't have anyone to show my view to. I don't have anyone to show anything to. That's all it is. Who can I show this picture to? Who can I play this song to? It is the one thing that feels lost about my retreat into myself.

Accepting – and it is hard and not done yet – that something exists because *I* look at it, because I see it, I hear it. There are things to which I alone will be witness. That is a responsibility and with that responsibility a loneliness, like all responsibilities – be it the itemised bill or saving the world, the divorcee and the Bat Hero are both lonely, because the work we do cannot be shared. With great vulnerability comes great responsibility.

In the break between the two lockdowns, there were a few days when it was very hot. One particular day, my sister was worried how her baby would cope without air conditioning.

'Right,' I said. 'Don't fight me on this – I'm taking us to Blakes.'

I revel in living the life of having a lover without having the lover. Blakes is one of the most romantic hotels in the world – why shouldn't I arrive with a small kid, my sister and her baby, use the hotel in a new way and still end up feeling high! The expense was, of course, exorbitant, but it wasn't wasteful. We had the best time. On the way back, the taxi driver told me there was only one other person he'd ever driven from Blakes to deepest North London, and that was Amy Winehouse.

One day, I went to get cash out for the babysitter and I walked past a beautiful house with stained wood frames, purple flowers and stained-glass lotus windows, and I said out loud to it: 'You're very beautiful.' Bashfully and thankfully, as Ben did when he first saw me naked. It doesn't bother me that I am flirting with a house.

There was a night during lockdown when I had a terrible migraine. I put CJ in the shower, told her how to wash her own hair, then handed her a nightie, placed her on the bed, asked her to get under the covers and said, 'I can't. I'm so sorry, I have to lie down. You've gotta put yourself to bed tonight.' I went to my room and lay down, and at only six years old, she did what I asked of her. I got up at 5 a.m. recovered and there she was, asleep. I was amazed, proud, heartbroken . . .

Maybe my best moment in lockdown was accidentally getting a bit too high and standing on my roof terrace as the sky over Ally Pally shot lavender. Suddenly, there were black clouds moving fast and a news helicopter had to race away as a huge thunderstorm rolled in. All while the *great* part of 'November Rain' by Guns 'N' Roses blasted in my ears. And, significantly, especially when high, most of it is shit, but the end of it is *great*. I did a rain dance to the sky and the building and the helicopter. A dance in the style of prime Axl Rose, crossed with the style of a wrecked single mother who successfully rationed her weed gummies for just such an occasion.

In my soaked gummy reverie, it hit me that all of those men I followed across countries have been the smartphone in which I lose myself. I'd scrolled through them until I found something that made me feel bad about myself. But now I have looked up finally and am amazed there is an outside world of trees and then embarrassed I could have forgotten they were there, and then excited to watch them.

The gummy kicked in deeper and it turned out: I am the trees! You can't see the wood for the trees. You can't see the trees for the smartphone. You can't see yourself for the men you've loved. You might not be into men. *You know what I mean.*

This beautiful divorce, this beautiful baby, this beautiful life. This life that from some angles has cheekbones and a tiny waist, perky seventies breasts, and from others is worn down, pale, pandemic roots, middle-aged spread – what do they expect us to do if not spread?! It doesn't make sense to get smaller as we know more.

On my roof, dancing to 'November Rain' while high, storms gathering, helicopters answering a call to a gang-stabbing, during a pandemic, with my exes watching in spirit – *that* is the best sex I have had in years.

Alongside the hideousness of the slogan 'Make America Great Again' (MAGA), I think of Tom Petty's line in 'Learning to Fly': 'Well, the good ol' days may not return.' Whatever you thought might one day come back, it isn't. And knowing and living with that is what makes you a whole human being. MAGA is so disturbing because there is sickness to any instance of nostalgia not used in the image of beauty.

When my mother dies, I won't get her back. It is unfathomable. But it is the truth. I accept that once a week, I'll cry about Tom Petty dying – because I am actually crying about the times when life isn't fair and the good don't win and the person who deserves to pull through doesn't. Because the parental unit cannot be put back together no matter how much the child – in their beauty and wonder and sorrow, their sweet paper dolls and their righteous anger – wants it so. Because it didn't go the way it should have. And the reason I can live with that is because before the unfairness, and after the death, the song is still there.

When the US election was finally called by CNN, Ben rings right away.

'Are you watching?'

Down the phone, he blasts 'The Payback' by James Brown. I blast 'Na Na Hey Hey Kiss Him Goodbye' by Steam.

His other line goes off and I hear him say, 'Paula, I'll call you back! No, I'll call you back.'

It's that awful English time of year when it's dark at 4 p.m. But I remind myself that's only for five weeks. Then it will start getting lighter.

'Ben? Call Paula back – I've got to make CJ's bunny pasta.'

He's carried these bunny pastas for his daughter from America in their own entire suitcase each time he's come to London. I hang up so he can call Paula. And I go and make the bunny pasta. It's a cool shape (like the new shape of us).

I started this part with a Tom Petty song and I'll continue on that path. In the video for 'Free Fallin'', the out-of-place heroine finds contentment and serenity while skateboarding in slow motion. My presidential term has been the search to become my own slow-motion effect. To hold for as long as I'm able the moments in the sky before I land. To stop harbouring resentment against the ground for pulling me back to earth.

From my top-floor attic, I so often find myself caught off guard by the sight of the moon and exclaiming, 'You're so fucking gorgeous!' As I'd first dreamed men would, when I was an adolescent looking at my reflection. So now I am him and the moon is me. And I am turned on. And I am sated.

It is a peaceful transfer of power.

Part Eight

After that November lockdown, as the pandemic still raged, Ben called from America and asked if he could quarantine in my attic, starting a film in Italy once he emerged. Working Title Films would give him £2000 to cover accommodation and since I had provided it, he'd transfer that fee to me. It was an interesting coda, given that his upset during the divorce had been about the finances.

How much would you have to be paid to share your sacred nest with your ex-husband the year of the deadliest pandemic in a hundred years, after you spent all of 2016 praying either you or he would die? Two thousand pounds, transferred to you by Working Title Films.

And it would be fine. Because things were different now. We had grown, both of us. It would all be absolutely OK. Think how happy it would make our daughter!

It's just I don't sleep more than two hours a night, in the week before he arrives.

The plan was that he'd spend Christmas with us before heading on to his next film. I was self-conscious because I'd gained weight in lockdown and though he'd had many girlfriends since our break-up, the consistent is: I find him easiest to get along with when he thinks I look desirable. We never do anything, but the possibility that we could, if we wanted, is helpful.

If there was no frisson between us, if I now looked like a mother instead of a young woman he found attractive *and* was failing as a mother? If I looked like a mother but I wasn't doing it right . . . ? I was a bag of nerves. Which read differently with the extra weight.

Prepping for his arrival, I went down to take out the cat litter. As I opened the door, I found him smoking on my doorstep and let out a scream. He hissed 'Jesus Christ, woman!' I stepped back – he seemed to be wearing Lana Turner's blue velvet turban. The ground-floor neighbour came out to check the source of the scream.

'Are you OK?'

'Completely fine. So sorry, that's my daughter's father.'

That sounded less activating than ex-husband (for the neighbour or for me?).

'What's for dinner?' Ben asked as he carried his bags up the stairs.

I immediately saw that he'd gained quite a large amount of weight. In case things went south, which they quickly can with us, I had a story in my back pocket. I mean, literally: I'd clipped out the newspaper story of Tony Hadley from Spandau Ballet personally intervening on behalf of a man who lost a game show owing to a question about pronouncing the singer's name (Hadley stepped in to say the contestant had it right and deserved the cash prize). I'd further prepared another news cut-out: the tale of Tony Mortimer from East 17 who, having never read a full book, started reading in lockdown.

As I turned on the oven, I heard Ben running the shower. He'd left the door ajar so I could hear and see him, naked, trilling to his naked form in the mirror, with something approaching delight: 'Oh what a fat fuck! What a fat fuck! Hooray! Hooray! He's a very, very sexy fat fuck!'

By bedtime, he was in a sulk with me. I did not feed him enough.

'You never feed me enough. You never have.'

I thought on my feet.

'Tony Mortimer . . .' I ventured.

'Yes?'

'From East 17 . . .' I continued.

'Yes . . . ? Get on with it, Fozzy! Fuck's sake!'

'He fell in love with reading in lockdown, having never finished a book. Now he loves reading.'

I brought out the actual newspaper clipping, because I know he didn't, at his very core, trust me.

Ben looked at the clipping, his round blue eyes brimming. His face contorted. He took a breath.

'That's very beautiful.' He wiped the tears from his cheeks.

I kept the Tony Hadley story safely in my back pocket in case I needed it.

One day, as we walked to the shops, he stood with his *Crocodile Dundee* hat waiting for the lights to change at the corner of the street, singing in a thick Aussie accent about a coronavirus character he invented: 'Covie Jack! Covie Jack! Covie Covie Covie Jack!' It remains unclear if Covie Jack was, like Typhoid Mary, a spreader, or more akin to a *Quigley Down Under*, some kind of heroic antivirus fighter.

I know my ex-husband so well that most of the time I can manage to translate for him. Actors' names, for example. When he recommends that a role I'm writing be offered to 'Chloe Murray', I know he means Chloë Moretz, and when he describes a film he's seen with the late Australian soap star 'Dieter Brunner', I know he in fact means German actor Daniel Brühl.

We all need one person in our immediate family who can translate our difficulties for us. It's my dad I called when, spinning her finger in a circle, CJ asked: 'What's that thing from the olden days that goes "whoooo!"?' My dad answered without looking up from his *New Yorker* magazine: 'A tornado.' I am so grateful Ben let us move close to them.

Unfortunately, Ben also spent much of each evening bellowing versions of 'Shout' by Tears For Fears, P.M. Dawn's only hit and 'A Hard Day's Night' by The Beatles – all rendered in the style of Australian campfire songs. They echoed around the small flat while he remained unseen, a voice at the top of my handmade spiral staircase. At a certain hour, Brazil awoke and he and Paula chatted, their conversations audible from every corner of the flat.

One day, we had a devastating fight about the theme song to the mid-70s sitcom *Welcome Back Kotter* and each went to our separate rooms. The next day, he confessed that I made him cry. We got along well until the moment we triggered each other, even three years after our divorce came through.

The next night, when Brazil awoke, I heard him being introduced to his girlfriend's grandmother. Even I – who made peace with him dating a 21-year-old girl who had once been my fan – have to admit: it was weird trying to impress your new girlfriend's grandma by FaceTime in your ex-wife's flat. For some reason, and it was instinctive, Grandmas cross a line.

I remember how hard he worked on mine. How he wore a trilby hat – I think to impress her – and removed it to tip it at her respectfully. And how she boomed: 'Will you kindly take your hat *orf* my dining table!' She was born two years after the last pandemic and died two years before this one.

The grandma intro is the only time I was actively disruptive. I agreed to CJ's request to play The Beatles ('Get Back', totally reasonable) and she shouted, 'I love Billy Preston!' She was seven years old – and I was too involved in my attempted disruption to pause and voice astonishment at her knowledge. Then she asked for 'I Got My Mind Set On You' by George Harrison – less reasonable, but I allowed it. At peak volume, which is upsetting for me, it's a pretty bad song, except it must have upset Ben more, so that was good. But when it ended he sounded fine. They were laughing together, he and his girlfriend and his girlfriend's grandma – Oh! how they laughed . . .

He finally hung up and came downstairs smiling because the introduction had gone so well. I looked at him. He looked at me. For a moment I was scared he was going to ask if he could buy me some Balenciaga sock shoes. Then he found his thought:

'Emmy? What's for dinner?'

Some years ago, we were trapped together: by an oath, our parental responsibility, our financial intertwinings and our very real love. We could not have foretold getting past that – having the courage to let go and then getting trapped together in a small flat by the pandemic. But there we were: right before Christmas, when he was meant to reach the end of two just-bearable weeks, London went into Tier 4. He couldn't leave.

Not knowing if he would definitely go, not knowing how, I felt unsettled. I found myself remembering things I'd long pushed away, the bad parts of LA sliding under the front door of my North London flat.

I documented the incremental incursions into my kingdom that had taken place before the divorce. I could make a map of both them and my participation. But the clearest in my head is this: when he was working in London without me, he accidentally linked his new iPad to our daughter's and all of his texts started popping through as she watched *The Octonauts*. I let him know I was seeing things I shouldn't see. By the time he was on a plane home to LA, I was at a divorce lawyer.

I called my best guy friend, Seamus, beside myself. His advice was fascinating.

'If you can find a way not to get divorced, then don't.'

Una threw her arms around me.

'You're Rita Marley! He'll always come back to you!'

My lip quivered as it dawned on me: 'But I want to be Bob.'

Ben landed, arriving at our door with a huge Gucci scarf for me: beige, edged in scarlet, printed with red blossom. Good, I thought. I deserve it. That was a very bad week and the scarf was a symbol of it. And, at the same time, I loved the scarf for what it was: soft and comforting and beautiful.

The next year, things had further devolved, we no longer shared a bed and, one evening after Una had left, he made an offer. He would stay if he could be allowed other women. And I looked at our kid, in her one-piece jammies, playing Lego – how happy she was that we were both there . . . And I said, 'OK, but you have to keep it from me.'

He didn't destroy me by asking. A lot of couples have arrangements. I destroyed myself by saying OK, which was worse than 'yes'. That's how Jefferson Airplane eventually became Starship. By agreeing to changes that stripped them of their fundamental identity.

'How would you feel if I was seeing other men?' I asked in a small voice.

His answer was instant.

'I'd be so relieved.'

When he said that, I wished I could just be dead, but I knew that I couldn't, because of my child – that I could have neither the death nor even the wish.

I felt like I had internalised all that was dangerous about living in California. Inside me was landslide and brushfire season and the possibility of how very long it had been since a serious earthquake.

I had not said what I wanted. Not at all. And that was on me. But it didn't matter anyway, because he kept forgetting the part about making sure to keep it secret from me.

'You seem like you are dying in little pieces,' said a friend. 'I can't feel you any more.'

I thought right away of Petty, of Alice in Wonderland and his refrain, 'I don't feel you any more.' I couldn't even look at my friend as I answered: 'I know,' I said. 'I know.'

I think now of the household spiders that ritually emerge from their hiding places every September, looking for other spiders to hug and kiss. And because they have no dating apps, they actually have to present themselves, in all their vulnerability. And when they do, people scream and try to squash them. That's how I think of our doomed marriage when I'm trying to see it from Ben's perspective. When he was trying to tell me who I was, he was only describing his own worst fears. But I did the same to him.

I know, alone in the LA family home, he still looks at the Australian animals mural I had painted in CJ's nursery and that as he does so, he understands what I tried to do and what I was reaching for. I look through the box of rings he gave me and feel the same of him.

I desperately wanted to write about everything his entrapment with us was bringing up, but I couldn't because he was sleeping in my office.

They creep inside you, the words from the past, like a stream of biting ants, and you try to wash them away. But even if you get rid of them, just that they made it into you, however briefly, is near impossible to scour from your heart.

It would take a long time. It might take abstaining from sex for years, completely, until you felt you had a clean slate. Not a slate: a room correctly equipped to record your own desires, without picking up all the passing vibrations that belong to other people.

Then, the most transgressive trampling of all possible boundaries occurred. I walked up to where he was playing a video game, thunder on my face. Even Ben looked scared.

'Foz?'

It took a moment to get the words out.

'Jake Tapper tweeted about you.'

'What?'

273

'Jake. Tapper. Of CNN. Tweeted. About. *You.*'

Only to admire his performance in a film, but still – it was an unfortunate birthday development.

A benefit of his extended stay is it bled into the week I had to have surgery on one eye and he was able to watch CJ. The day of the surgery, I was fine. But by the next day, when the anaesthesia had worn off, I felt terrible, unbalanced. I heard the death thoughts for the first time in almost twenty years. I knew they were a mirage resulting from heavy drugs, but that they could even be conjured – that the raw materials existed – was incredibly disturbing to me. This lockdown *would* end, he would be gone. I would be alone with her again. But, under the influence, it didn't feel that way. I was very frightened and that wasn't something I'd felt since it became my job, alone, to keep her safe.

In the age of the heroic vaccine, what could be done for me to prevent this? Why has there never been a vaccine against madness? I guess because, if there was, the mad people would say it was a conspiracy and refuse to take it.

The single most notable way my world has shrunk since I became a mother and a single mother at that is I no longer have the freedom to dream into death. I miss it very badly some nights, those times I have no choice but to feel all the feelings and know and accept how hard the road ahead is and that it might not be exciting and heart breaking, some of it is going to be boring and heart breaking.

The mantra 'I wish I were dead' floats back to me – not because I wish I were, but because it's a sign I've seen printed so often in the background of my brain. Like 'We

Buy Gold' in the Lower East Side of New York or 'Choking Victim' in a restaurant.

After the surgery and the panic, something unusual happened to bring me back: I couldn't get in the shower for five days and Ben offered to wash my hair for me. He did so beautifully, with great care.

'Does your neck feel OK?' he asked as he massaged my scalp with the suds.

He was so kind and gentle – the closest act of intimacy we'd had in many years. It was almost . . . almost like how we used to make love when we first got together.

The next morning, when I crept up the spiral staircase to see if he was awake, I found that he'd fallen asleep with his iPad on his chest and Paula, beamed from a bedroom in Brazil, asleep on the screen. They must spend each night falling asleep this way . . .

Although she was on an iPad, she still felt vulnerable to me. Even so, I couldn't help but take a look. When I did, I saw: she was just a girl. Not a beautiful Brazilian model, not a temptress and a heartache, but a girl who was just pretty enough, who could bend and shape it into something gorgeous and on a bad day not. In other words, a girl like me. She was the age I was when I first left the city I'd been shamed by.

Feeling protective of her, I crept out, gently, so as not to disturb their reverie.

I have never written the phrase 'trigger warning', but this is a sexual abuse trigger warning for the next paragraph.

The morning Ben was finally able to leave, the papers in both America and here reported the execution of Lisa Montgomery – the first woman to be federally executed in seventy years. After a lifetime of extreme sadistic sexual abuse that began in early childhood and continued through her marriage, in a state of complete disassociation, she committed a terrible murder. I'd followed the case closely and prayed for her each night. The Trump administration expedited her killing, made sure there was no stay, knowing the man who would take office in seven days was a religious Catholic, staunchly anti the death penalty. They did it as fast as they could.

I felt like I needed to collapse into Ben's arms, but I could smell his cigarette and hear his podcast. He asked for coffee and I knew those weren't my arms to collapse into any more.

That I'd known so much comparable peace and had so much comparable power in my life, left me even more devastated for a woman who left the planet without having a single moment of either. That I got to choose to start sex, and I got to choose to stop sex – *I* had choice. I had sorrow from it and adventure and beauty from it. This woman. This woman . . . It was one of the worst things I could remember hearing in my life.

A few hours later, when Ben finally left for the airport, he hugged me and thanked me sincerely.

'I hope you know . . . I hope you know how much it means to me . . .' His round blue eyes searched mine. 'That you let me stay in this family.'

I was touched.

Once he was in his limo heading for the airport, I went upstairs to where he'd been staying. I wanted to write in my clean white rooftop space – the only room in this flat I'd left empty of possessions, the better to write. But I couldn't get to my desk. Everywhere I looked, there were half-bottles of Lucozade, cigarette boxes, lighters, discarded tins of Ovaltine. The gift I gave him and the gift that my parents gave him for Christmas had been abandoned where they were first opened. There were stacks of books he'd bought (Bob Woodward and atlases, that brilliant mind ticking over) – and also sinus inhalers, tubs of cheap hand cream.

An expensive Margiela white towel, covered in coffee stains. Pairs of his drug-store reading glasses, broken pencils, After Eight wrappers, showered around the bed like confetti. Incense, cotton buds (some unused, some used). My pale pink satin comforter, now studded with cigarette burns.

Red Post-it notes were affixed to the slanted ceiling above my desk, biro'd with words I had to climb over

Part Nine

When I was writing this book and I couldn't escape my ex-husband, I checked into a hotel that was surviving Tier 4 by renting day rooms as offices. It was OK – I wedged the desk at an angle and had a quarter view. The next day, a family vacated and they moved me to a suite on the top floor.

The view was of blue sky and rooftops and chimneys. It was so lovely and the hotel was so deserted, that I had the overwhelming urge to have sex. I didn't think about who the partner might be. The part I kept thinking about was how, after being satisfied in the afternoon, I would get up from whoever it was, gather the sheets around me, with a cup of tea or a joint, walk to the window and look out at that skyline.

I picture having a long day's work in my top-floor flat – resting and reading and writing. And at the end of the day, when the sun turned down and dusk fell, I visualise changing my clothes and a man coming to my door. But in both cases the sexual fantasy is dependent on first having my time alone, or it doesn't light my fire.

Maybe I'm a witch. I fit the archetypal description. There was no man and I didn't need one. I'd soon reach the end of my childbearing years and I had never felt so powerful. But without the moon, I wondered if there would be enough light for me to see how much I have. I was a single mum who used to be sixteen and was now forty-two. I weighed so much less than I did in my twenties. I wasn't fat then, I was just full, so full. Now I was a waning moon. But, if you believe in such things, waning moons are good for bringing spells to fruition.

'Why are you so old?' my daughter asked one day, not meaning to be rude.

I stroked her ears, considering. 'I think because . . . I'm still alive?'

The moon was waxing gibbous as I wrote this, sliced like a wedding cake, that orange almond taste in the skies.

Sometime after telling me I had his favourite constellation on my face, Adam Yauch died very young. Even now, I remember him for seeing me, for telling me I had power, while men were already trying – with words and actions that would go on for many years – to take it away.

In his memory, there's the Adam Yauch playground in Brooklyn. And a middle-aged woman in North London, Pleiades beneath her left eye, saying to herself, 'Look up. Look up.'

That's her! That's her – Emma Forrest in middle age reflected in the glass of a shop window! Nobody is looking at her unless to be annoyed that she's in their way. But I was so fond of myself, so happy to live inside my body with her. So grateful that she was the one I cried for.

I waited for the traffic lights to change at the junction, walked past the petrol station. I noticed they had changed it to a Waitrose from a Budgens and I felt life looking up. And I also badly missed my grandma, who exclusively shopped at Budgens.

Then the stairs up into my flat. Stairs up and up and up. And into my space that came from his mother who did not manage to survive what I did survive. And the bespoke spiral staircase did look beautiful. It was there to keep me safe, but from a specific angle you could fall to your death. It was an item that was necessary for me to create. It led me on a path to my best work.

How beautiful it was from there. And it was not fair that this was all we got. It wasn't fair and yet I loved it there so much. It wasn't fair to Ben that I 'got' half of the proceeds from his mother's flat sale. To the core of his being, it was an injustice. And in the end, what's absolutely not fair will absolutely set you free.

I was about to move again. Because of the pandemic, I had taken a rental for a year in a place that has a garden. I would rent mine out to another writer. I thought I'd get quality time in my old flat to think, but of course I wouldn't – the quality time had already happened. I was packing like crazy, but lying down on the couch in which Ben made his nest, I rested a few minutes, then opened my eyes, looking out at the night-time view. So beautiful. Really as unbelievable as our LA view, though that was a mansion and this is a top-floor flat. I'd come to love it here so much that I was only leaving for my daughter, to give her outdoor space.

I would walk down the spiral staircase crafted for safety and beauty. I would be safe. I would lock the door. I was safe. She who cut herself, who wounded herself, who was so ashamed of herself, who had needed a husband to protect her from the past.

I was safe.

＊

North London on a rainy morning: an old lady was delicately navigating the rain with geisha steps, a clear umbrella over her. I could see she'd done her white hair in waves and she was wearing bright lipstick. A young man pushed past her, his shoulder catching her painfully. She turned to him as he swaggered on. He walked back towards her, agitated, asking in pub-fight tones: 'What? You got something to say?'

She could see he was bigger than her, but what I could pick out from my position further away was that he was crazy. As he got closer, she registered the twitch and the aggression, faltered. And when he demanded again, '*What?*', she said quietly, '*I am here.*'

I waited to make sure he kept moving, that he didn't follow her, and then cried all the way home.

Even in the face of the mad, the broken, the dismissive, the irreparably damaged, even if they can't hear you because there is so much interior distortion it effects their brain waves and their body movements, *it matters*, saying out loud, 'I am here.' Especially for women. Especially as we are deemed, with each passing decade, to be of diminishing value. Because someone who is that crazy, someone who takes beyond their fair share with their broken energy, cannot be the one to tell you you no longer exist.

My version of 'I am here' was texting a man a photograph of a cat who looked like the actor Ron Perlman. I considered sending it to Ben, but willed myself not to, since he never checks texts or emails and because we are not technically in a relationship. I'd been overwhelmed for almost a year by having no one I could send this photograph to, just occasionally taking out my phone and looking at it, mournfully, by myself. That was the sign that perhaps I might want to consider dating someone. The picture burned in my pocket, quite separate from a desire for sexual congress. It was there so long that in that period even *Ron Perlman* got divorced and began a new relationship.

The man I texted it to appreciated it. He wasn't beside himself with delight, he did not split his sides, but he seemed amused enough. Because I am writing this in 2021, I, of course, hadn't met him yet. *The algorithm concept is strange.* I didn't say I was looking for someone courtly but mischievous – there was nowhere to say it unless through my clothes and hair and eyes and music choices. So maybe I did say it. Because that's who I got matched with.

We wrote back and forth and it was easy. He made me smile and sometimes laugh. I liked his profile picture a lot, in which he grinned beside a stabled horse. I enjoyed talking to him enough that I mentioned him to Ben, who studied the profile picture and approved.

'Clever boy: he's telling the world he's got a big cock.'

'He is not saying that! He's telling the world that he likes animals.'

'No,' said my ex-husband, in the same decisive tone he'd use as he handed a bewildered grocery-store worker an orange he considered overripe. Just 'No,' he said as he placed it in their hands and continued up the aisle.

My match was a lot younger than me, but it was an age gap that means that while I could *technically* be his mother, I'd be such a young mum, it would cause a great deal of family strife and societal judgement. It might even receive a condemnation from Sarah Vine in her *Mail On Sunday* column.

Then the young man sent me a piece of music. I was just learning these things: that you could send each other Voice Notes and link it to favourite tracks via Spotify. He'd already sent me several and at the start, my dazzling spotlight not fully trained on him yet, I probably skipped over one or two. This one was 'Anemone' by The Brian Jonestown Massacre. Though he might have sent it because it's one from my era, it was actually a song I'd never heard. And a weird thing happened. I was listening to it, the house quiet. I guess I was a little high on a gummy I found in my handbag when I was looking for a dry-cleaning ticket and the song flooded my body until I had to pull my jeans off. Before the song was over, I could feel this man I hadn't seen in person yet sliding inside me. It was pretty easy to say yes to meeting after that. I believe I was the one to make the suggestion.

We were going to meet outside on a park bench, but then we didn't because – and I believe this was also my idea – there was something about the rain. Too much or not enough, or it might have been the wrong density.

Two mothers from school helped me, Aoife by watching my kid and Dani by coming over to let me take my clothes off in front of her so she could check whether or not my body had become disgusting in the years since anyone had seen it.

On my way over I thought that if this was no good and my masturbatory hunch was wrong, at least I got a song out of it. How amazing to get to my forties, to have seen so many shows and bought so many albums, and still there were songs I didn't know. To think that, after such a big life, there wasn't a finite set of musical notes in my iPod, in my capabilities . . . We always ask ourselves, 'Is there more to this?' – to alien life, to motherhood, to our career – and a great song we've never heard says, 'Well, *yeah*.'

All those years untouched had filled me with a palpable power. It was infinite. It was regenerating, even right now, and I had to be left untouched to do that. But I needed to know I could let someone inside me – even for a little while, even for some nights – and it wouldn't take away my power. That can't happen again. And getting myself back to a place where I could safely let a man inside would take as long as it took.

You can't keep opening the oven door to check. It's a slow bake. You'll know. You'll take a toothpick and it will come out clear and it will be ready. And then you can eat yourself.

So I listened to this song he gave me – I could say 'sent', but it feels like 'gave', like a letter with a family insignia stamped into a wax seal. And then I went there, the compass magnetising my cab from the north to the south. And I saw us already as rulers of different lands and one of us was going to have to bend the knee, and *that* was a turn-on, too.

When he opened the door, he looked displeased to see me, and I thought: fuck you – now I'm going to kiss you. A 'fuck-you' kiss is very different from a 'hate fuck'. It's a means of taking control of a situation, not dissimilar from directing. Then I realised he was just slightly anxious, so, after I'd kissed him, I sat beside him and waited for him to gain the courage to look at me. Once he looked, he didn't look away. It wasn't long before he overcame any anxiety he may have harboured and removed my underwear with his teeth.

A presidential term can end quickly and decisively, just like it did in real life. Were those long years really a thirty-second dream? We waited so long for a Republican to say of Trump: 'Here is the line he has crossed – we are done with him.' But they never did. But there, you see, my underwear was on the floor: *this crosses a line.*

The young man was sexually intuitive, filthy and communicative – everything sex should be for. A communion when there aren't the words. After all, how could there be the words when we didn't know each other yet?

It was of the highest imperative to have him inside me, but he wouldn't let me yet – 'Not yet' – and instead he made me come with his tongue. To try to get my breath back, I found myself making the Scarlet Witch's hand movements in the air before I was able to sit up again. Having watched every episode of *WandaVision* together, she was there and not there – my child. All those hours and weeks and months and years as a mother and not a woman, from the time Ben and I stopped having sex, from the end of the marriage in the City of Love. She may not have planned to, but my daughter had given me space. She is generous – she would find a way to be OK with it if I decided it was the right time to take a lover.

We talked easily afterwards and I quickly sensed I had returned to Britain to have celibacy ended by a man who could only possibly be from here, his energy invested with Bryan Ferry, Jarvis Cocker, Peter Cook, Gilbert & George – an unusual combination of both fussy and free. And then I understood what I'd done: instead of falling for James Bond, I'd fallen for Q. '*You're so strange!*' I marvelled, and Q agreed that he was. He whispered in my ear a series of questions and it was the first non-draining questionnaire I had responded to since I got pregnant: Would you like it if I . . .? Would you like it if I . . .? Yes, please. No, thank you – I am vegetarian. We talked about next time, about latex and zips and spanking, role play, which of us deserved to be punished and why and how and when.

He could not know how many times over how many years since my daughter was born I've been scratched, bitten, pinched, as all mothers have, and how much it meant to have him use my body for something else. That I wanted to be smacked – but only because I asked to be smacked, not because I failed to duck a flying hardback of *Roald Dahl's Marvellous Joke Book*.

Q leaned in and asked, 'What would I do to you in your wildest imagination?'

I immediately answered, 'You'd put a song inside me.'

I suppose what I was saying is that I wanted him like I wanted music through headphones. For him to be inside only me: to override the female conundrum and allow me to disappear, again and again and again, without making me lose myself.

But I was not free to stay in this room and never leave. I had responsibilities, to which I rode home in a black taxi, crossing the bridge as the sun was beginning to set. I returned from the south to the north, wiped. The whole afternoon was like the gummy I found in my bag when I was looking for a dry-cleaning ticket, so I couldn't even remember what bridge the cab crossed over.

But all bridges are beautiful to look at and all bridges are dangerous for women walking along them. To be a woman is a balance between how much we want to have sex with a particular person and how our greatest fear is having sex against our will with a stranger. Sex can bring us closer to ourselves and sex can dissect us from ourselves. It contains, within its possibilities, total freedom and absolute fear.

I listened to a Hanukkah mix tape my mum made for me twenty years earlier, a single song I was to hear per night, each one she'd chosen as favourite and meaningful.

What did my mum make of mothering? She who had been a glamorous career woman high up in advertising, saying she couldn't understand why if there were two parents, she was always putting both coats on both children. When my sister and I asked her why she wanted to be with our dad, who was a lot younger than her and just starting his career, she'd answered that she thought he was very sexy and we'd just looked at each other in shock that she could feel that, that *he* might have been that.

I hope Mum never reads this book, but I'm glad she can still be there with me in this world beside the other world (the sex world), and that makes me believe she will still be felt when she's gone.

You know who was not in that room? Ben. Nowhere. Completely overridden by a 27-year-old. Which either makes me fickle or Q very powerful.

I got home and changed. When I took off my tights, I discovered they smelled of him, so I huffed my own lingerie, steadying myself against the sink because his scent, combined with mine, was so intoxicating. I am my own pervert. *Good.*

Later that evening, when the taxi had returned me from the South London flat to my suburban North London home, Ben tried to FaceTime our daughter who still wasn't back.

I hid my mouth, which was badly swollen from kisses and bites, but he got it out of me.

'What's going on?'

'Nothing.'

'It doesn't look like nothing.'

'I had my first sexual experience since we split, OK?'

'Oh, Fozzy! Was it good?'

'It was fuckin' great.'

He narrowed his eyes. 'So, is he big?'

'Yeah. He is.'

Ben started crying, tears of joy running down his sharp cheekbones.

'I'm so happy for you, Fozzy,' he sniffed. 'I want the mother of my child to be getting deep dick.'

I turn on the dishwasher.

'Thank you, Ben.'

'But. *But*, if he hurts the mother of my child'– he made his terrible Melbourne Sharpies face, with lips peeled back and vile little smokers' teeth exposed – 'I will fucking kill him.'

'I know.'

And I think it was at least half true, because he was so relieved not to be the villain that he took to villainising another man with gusto. I knew, because I'd do exactly the same.

I looked at the time on the oven – all these machines of domesticity.

'Shit! She'll be back from her play date any minute. Shit, my fucking lip!'

'Fozzy, chill out. She doesn't know what you've done. You deserve this and your child can't see into your soul.'

He only thought that because he was not her primary carer.

The next time I left the house to meet Q, my daughter had become alert to something happening that she wasn't in on. As I exited, she made a point of saying, 'You look horrible.'

'Thanks,' I said.

'And you smell bad.'

'Cool!'

'And you are a very bad writer. *Golden* is the worst book I ever read.'

(She means my novel *Royals*, whose title is embossed on its cover in gold and that she has not read).

I was touched that she understood how much my writing means to me. God, I love that kid, with her halo of charm. I notice children in playgrounds who are charmless and, though it doesn't make them bad people, it does exacerbate how boring parenting can be. CJ, more often than not, interests me.

'I'll see you in the morning, darling!'

I tried to hug her but she turned away.

As I waited for Q at the hotel, CJ FaceTimed me in tears. Q kept texting his ETA and saying how much he wanted me. Right as I could hear the elevator doors open and his footsteps moving up the hall, CJ pointed her finger at me through the screen and hissed, '*You and I shall never separate!*'

Shaken by what appeared to be a witch's curse, I lay down the phone and opened the door.

Later that night, I showed Q the film that means the most, that I've seen the most, but we didn't finish it because we were tired from fucking. But then as we were dropping off, we recovered long enough to fuck again. Then we woke the next day and did it twice more. In telling him he's by far the best lover I'd ever had, it later occurred to me that though it was true, I also have the tone of a very proud mother who thinks their kid was the best in the school play.

He texted 'I think this is a song you'd like,' and a link to 'Sweet Harmony' by The Beloved, which I'd listened to, over and over, in my bedroom as a kid who wished she was dead. It was then I realised: he was born when things started to go wrong for me. It was a facet in why he tugged at my heart. His strangeness, his physical beauty, his curious mind, the fact he was the first in five years – they all matter, yes. But that childhood bedroom was so bad, all alone. That pain was so real. The wishing there was someone out there to feel connected to felt so hopeless. Then thirty years later, this boy thought I might like the song.

He was right. I didn't even tell him how I had it on cassette tape single. How would I have explained the concept? How do you explain any of it? Explaining what a cassette tape single was felt no bigger or smaller than trying to explain divorce or failure, or sexual assault. They *all* hurt to think about. All of them.

During the week, I was astounded by his sexts. Not so much getting off to them as parsing them like symbols from alien life.

I showed Dani my most treasured among them on the walk back from school drop-off.

She nodded. 'That's good. I mean it's a great thought and solid writing. What did you say back?'

I told her: that I wished I could keep some of his semen in a locket so I could always taste him.

Dani stopped dead in the street.

'Right. That's interesting. And how did he take that?'

'I mean, I haven't done this in a long time. It's what came to mind. It's not like I said, "I want to store your semen in Bob Dylan's attachable harmonica holder so I can play guitar while tasting you."'

And she laughs until a little bit of wee comes out. I love it when my friends laugh at me. Not with me, but at me. It brings me the same flavour of pleasure as being spanked.

The first time Q and I booked dinner out together, I was at the table, reading my *New Yorker*, when he texted:

> All I can say in excuse for my lateness is that I do look
> like a handsome 27-year-old man who smells nice.

And I thought, how interesting: there seemed to be an unspoken agreement that it was him whose attractiveness we were gathering to venerate. Like the sixties films where Terence Stamp and Warren Beatty were lit with the same, if not greater, degree of care than Julie Christie and Natalie Wood.

I noticed, with him on my mind, that I'd started buying clothes again. So many. I bought them specifically because I could imagine them being removed. Nothing that was too hard to take off. I was drawn to them not by whether they were fashionable, but whether they could be easily raised and the way they'd sit when they were. *That* can be slipped down. *That* would look good on the floor, a cape covering a puddle of what I was, to step over who I used to be.

Now I was having sex again, I found myself into porn for the first time since I was pregnant, which was the only other time I'd ever watched it. There's a girl on Kink.com who is my favourite. I feel her. 'I feel you,' we say when we want someone to know they're being listened to. And that makes a porn icon. Can you actually feel them? Do they seem like they're feeling anything? How do you know that, with all the plausible accusations of how damaging porn is to women, this is not horror and sorrow to them?

Then, for the first time, I noticed the multitude of white scars on the girl's upper thighs and I had to close the laptop. I took a breath and went back to look. They were neat, deliberate. The whiteness suggests they were two or three years old. I know the path of scars and I didn't see any fresh ones.

I know that girl. I remember her. She wanted to be obliterated from a young age. There was no one she could trust to do it, so there was nobody to do it but herself. Is this a step away from or towards destruction? If someone else is doing it to her, and it's role play, is she getting better? Is she safer, now she's using sex to try to vanish?

In the most common kink – S&M – you can be verbally abused, but it relies on near constant communication. You may be getting hurt, but you are not being ignored – and I think that's a childhood wound that participants are often seeking to heal. I had no boundaries growing up, because I was told I was too overpowering to implement rules with, and now I like to be submissive, it is comforting to me. It is, when I am connected to a lover, like a kitten being picked up by the scruff of their neck – how their whole face goes slack and relaxed.

There is, among all the other available search words on Kink, a category so morally corrupt, so triggering, a word that instantly floods me with shame when I see it: 'British'. I understand their point, that 'British' is in and of itself a perversion. But when you click on it, you're really just linked to one exceptionally loathsome middle-aged pig man. In every gang bang, he's by far the most aggressive (there's always one decent, usually younger man who breaks the fourth wall to check in on the girl's comfort). 'British' comes across as not only a sadist, but *also* like a middle manager at the EE mobile-phone shop, who won't serve you next even though you were clearly standing right there. There is no Kink channel for role-playing CNN news anchors, for whispering, 'You are being fucked by a Jew,' in Steve Bannon's blistered ear, or for making love to Senator John McCain's ghost.

Mainly, when I masturbate, I see Q, pale and angular and searching the way you only can with someone you don't know. He who pulled the drawbridge back down.

And there the problem strikes me: I couldn't keep think-ing of him as a stranger I had a fling with. I wanted to know him. The porn – reductive, impersonal – was me attempting to buffer the deep wanting sensation I felt when we weren't together – the bodily anxiety of being blown away by someone.

My body was trying to wrestle off sleep, the reactiva-tion of sex having triggered every nerve. It frightened me that, after all those years of abstinence, I exited it with no dimmer switch to my desire – that I only had 'off' or 'rail me'.

Another part of the white-hot desire was welded to the resentment I felt towards him for being able to go out whenever he wanted to go out, whereas for me it was a complex arrangement reliant on generous sleepover invites or babysitter fees. It was easy for him to cancel, too, which was not done with any malice; though nor was it done with thoughtfulness.

I told him the Bette Midler story and he was confused.

'Who is Bette Midler?'

At first I thought he was joking, but then I saw him googling her.

'Right,' he said, then looked up. 'Nobody had ever heard of Bette Midler until today.'

He talked frequently about consent, which was inter-esting for someone who was endlessly surprising me. I prepped – emotionally inoculating myself in the time of vaccination – that this would likely end and when it did, we could leave each other better than we found each other. You couldn't ask for more. You could, but you'd be wrong. The most commonly used quote by the spiritual teacher Ram Dass is 'Be here now,' but I am most attached to another of his, 'We're all just walking each other home.'

And when I am thinking of ways to steal away from my daughter so I can fix what I have to fix and forget what I yearn to forget, returning at night to the terror that she will one day know her own sexual shame. Statistically, this brave and beautiful girl cannot be protected and my best hope is that it will be the least damaging version of it.

I love her so much. I wanted him so much. I didn't know how to make maternal love and sexual longing sit well beside each other like Ben's crow's feet next to his boyish blue eyes or Q's dimples either side of his strong jaw.

I sent Q my first ever nude selfies. He didn't ask for them and responded with the same polite good cheer as he did the photograph of the Ron Perlman cat. But I liked to see myself in curious positions. The concept of the nude selfie provided the same hit for me as the teenage lists I made for my own funeral, with elaborate seating plans and order of speakers. Like fantasising about your own funeral, or giving yourself your own nickname, the nude selfie goes against reason: because you are *you*, these are not your photographs to take. But like all impossible things, it is enticing, and I kept circling back to it.

I wanted to ask him for a WhatsApp of his dick, with a newspaper showing the date so I knew it was taken for me – but then it might look like his penis was being held to ransom.

One morning, we woke in a hotel room overlooking a charming garden, watching the rain like cats. We stretched against each other and then away, and I felt quite calm. He put on 'Chain Reaction', the song Barry Gibb wrote for Diana Ross, which went to number one in the UK and Australia but was an abject failure in the US because, despite us all speaking the same language, America has periodic outbreaks of madness that can be very hard to understand. Prohibition, Trump, the anti-vax movement, the failure of 'Chain Reaction'.

'Barry's backing vocals are amazing. Are you ready, are you listening?' Q prodded me. 'It's about to be ultimate Barry . . . *There!*'

I thought, wow, you are very good at sex, but the way your buttons are pushed by Barry Gibb really has me all in.

I asked him to make me a playlist of songs about rain and I doubted he ever would, but that was where you got to keep your power, by asking for what you want, knowing you may not receive it.

The Covid-19 vaccine roll-out had finally reached Q's age group. I told him how in that first lockdown, I'd had sex dreams about Boris Johnson.

'I imagine they were about death,' I said. 'I could feel his hair in my hands, luminous and scratchy. I'd arrange it nicely, but it couldn't be made sense of.'

He sighed. 'In the first lockdown, every girl I'd ever dated wanted phone sex and to send me nudes. It was overwhelming. I could have opened a gallery. I wouldn't – that would be revenge porn. But I eventually stopped looking. I had sex with so many women at the start of the pandemic, it's like the Band Aid song: I couldn't tell you who did which part.'

Internally, I recoiled. Of course – this was generational. What was new frontier for a woman in her forties was yesterday's *repetitive* news to a man in his twenties.

After he left for work, I made a point of taking more photos, just for me, in the hotel mirror, the crumpled sheets visible in the frame. I could recoil at his sangfroid all I liked, but that did not undo last night's multiple orgasm.

'We get a picture of our love in motion!' is the awkward phrase in 'Chain Reaction', trilled lustily by Barry Gibb. It is ridiculous, absurd and transcendent.

I craved Q giving me back my body, on my own terms. Someone who could, once a week, make me shatter in a completely different way. But he didn't have once a week.

He had huge wants – and his own pain to sort through and career highs to come. I was one facet of this wanting – the time he dated an older woman. A stepping stone that got to shudder and explode when he was available to step on me. I was wet every time I let myself think about him for too long. But when I was celibate, I was the water. And part of me misses that.

Waiting to read his words, I recognised my liberal use of the WhatsApp 'mute' function (setting my phone so it wouldn't ping when he contacted me), then going into it to check if he had anyway. It reminded me of all the times I ever covered a plate of chips with a napkin to try to shield myself from temptation – the paper towel burka quickly lifted.

One afternoon, a day after he'd cancelled me late, I sat across his lap and leaned in to kiss him with lips chapped from a dry mouth from too many sleep medications and none of them working. I saw his glasses were Dolce &

Gabbana and it was interesting to notice glasses since it was a day when we saw clearly we were not the perfect match we had painted each other to be. And I remember talking with my LA therapist about the subtext in the Dolce ads, wanting to buy what they were selling via their recreation of Bardot imagery, if it meant carefree love then growing old with no one to observe but the animals you sheltered. I've always associated that ad with walking away from being a sexual being and choosing total solitude.

It can be fun to feel like you always see subtext. It can also not be fun.

The afternoon light in his bedroom did different things. Over the course of a month, it had changed and instead of making me feel like we made our own time, it made me feel inspected and exposed and chivvied. My breath tasted awful from the sleeping pills that didn't make me sleep, so imagine how I tasted to him . . . I hated that afternoon. He felt cold and the wrong kind of strange – and I hadn't had more than two hours' sleep a night in ten days.

After sex, in which I was too disconnected to come, he looked at his phone and said Helen McCrory was dead. It was a terrible ending to an afternoon that had got away from both of us. McCrory represented wit and passion, eroticism and mystery. A middle-aged woman at the peak of her powers and the sense it wasn't even a peak because she would only improve. You couldn't ask for a better role model for all we could be and all the power we could hold.

I sat on his doorstep waiting ten minutes for a cab that kept arriving then retreating, like love. By the time I got home, I was in a state. I had to hold it together because I'm a mum. I had to make her dinner and bathe her, put her pyjamas on, read her a story and put her to bed. Once she was asleep, I wanted to talk to him, but I couldn't because it was too early to let myself be broken with someone.

Why did this young man have this hold on me, if I knew it couldn't possibly be real love between us? What I did with him was the only place in my life completely untouched by any feelings of shame. It's funny that 'shameless!' is an insult. Because it's the greatest thing I could wish for a woman and I had it in bed, with him. And that feeling is intoxicating.

I've felt deep shame in conversations with my mother, who I love and who loves me. I've felt shame with my father. With my ex-husband. Definitely with my daughter, so haunted am I still by the morning of the paper dolls. I've felt it with every teacher I can remember. Every boyfriend. Every boyfriend's parents. My mother's friends. Newspaper editors. People I got too close to. People who knew to stay away from me. I truly think the only ones I've never felt shame with are the moon, my sister and hotel beds with Q.

To realise the tentacles of shame are all those places, beneath all those still surfaces – when I think of that, I break my own heart.

I felt very sad once I accepted that I was falling in love with Q and that he was not particularly available to me. So I did what men often do when they're overwhelmed by the feeling of being blown away by a woman. They have a one-night stand with someone new.

After we'd connected on the app, the message came:

Floored. Your playlist. You are cool as fuck.

Like Q, this young man seemed as drawn by my music as by me, which made me feel like an erotic Pied Piper.

What if I'm cooler than fuck?

He pinged back:

I apologise: it was wrong of me to limit the field of fuck . . .

And we talk the rest of the night.

In my Britpop youth, guys who were music obsessives were older and were constantly looking over your shoulder at parties, in a state of anxiety about whether or not Paul Weller might show up.

He was a music producer, 6 foot 4 and twenty-six, and I realised, for someone who failed their maths GCSE and then declined to resit it, I'd suddenly become interested in numbers. The weather was lovely at the park where we met and he was almost instantly his own person, very distinct from the one on whom I was trying not to fixate – a very different, very heady flavour. It wasn't right to call either a boy, as both had more self-confidence than any of the middle-aged men I'd known.

As we walked, I was already calculating how many kinds of ice cream I was allowed. Because I really wanted Q. I wanted him so bad I couldn't sleep. But now I wanted this one, too. To cross senses, I'd say Q was new wave, which is of course extremely sexy. The musician was on SRT (Standard Reggae Time). Though it could be the weed, he had a rhythm that made me feel heavy-lidded, as if I were moving in molasses.

The concept of dates is a US capitalist construct and I remain somewhat amazed that it had caught on in the UK in the time I'd been away. But he kept calling it a date. After paying our respects to Karl Marx at Highgate Cemetery, we walked up to Parliament Hill, where we lay on a blanket, vaping weed and stealing glances at each other's real-life profiles.

We played each other favourite tracks. I asked how he felt about Lana Del Rey, said that I was uninitiated until the latest album, which has a self-produced song with the lyric:

> I come from a small town, how 'bout you?
> I only mention it 'cause I'm ready to leave LA
> And I want you to come.

But in the production, as she sings the word 'want', underneath it she has looped the word '*need*', so you hear both the text and the subtext at the same time.

He pulled out his phone to play it under the big blue sky and, as the loop happened, he gasped. He, too, had never heard such a thing. It seemed like a signal just to tell the truth – a shot of music instead of a shot of tequila.

As we talked, finally, I could smell him. That would be the next vanguard of apps – if you could know their scent before you clicked. Now, I'd become half mother, half cat, hyper aware of both safety and scent. Now, I was a young girl, pressing herself against a father figure.

We kissed until secondary-school children pointed and laughed at us. (I remember being their age and wanting simultaneously both to be kissed and to make fun of people for kissing. I, too, am conflicted – amused by them and a little scared of them, because I can hear their voices but not see their faces.) We decided to go back to my old flat, which would be empty for one week before renters arrived. Q was meant to come see it, but he cancelled.

Exiting the park, we stopped to buy pasta at a deli – he'd lost his face mask in our kisses and I only had a lace Dita Von Teese one, which he didn't care about putting on and this touched me and turned me on.

I associate him with not only Lana Del Rey, but also staircases, since we could only make it to the first landing before falling into each other. Single motherhood is often hard and sometimes sad, and it was an enormous relief to be devoured. I think because he was so hungry, it spilled over and, the night and morning I was with him, I wanted to cook for him, which I never want to do, as my cooking is tied to implications of domestic failure and inability to be an obedient or successful housewife.

'What do you want me to do to you?' he asked after the sun had gone down.

These young men gauging your sexual pleasure! The men I dated at his age never asked you what you wanted or how to please you. You were just meant to be pleased to be chosen, validated that it was you on whom their gaze had, for now, fallen.

So what did I want him to do to me?

I thought, fleetingly, of the pretend husband who'd fleeced my bank account by telling the spiral staircase man that I was 'dippy'.

Then I told the musician I wanted him to tie me to the spiral stairs and let me watch him masturbate, and that he could touch me however he wanted. I handed him the beautiful Gucci scarf I was given by Ben as reparation. This wasn't on my vision board. I was just adjusting dialogue on the day to roll with a new direction.

The musician took the scarf and used it to tie my hands above my head to the banister. I felt like a carved mermaid on the front of a ship. I was my own pirate. He was a pirate I'd teamed up with.

The lights were gleaming through my huge rooftop windows. His chest was vast, like the sky in LA. The hilltop London view was beyond him. I felt awe, and like all moments of awe, it was the result of an experience outside my frame of reference.

The feeling of awe is controlled by the amygdala – the same part of your brain that detects threat and processes shock. The part of me that shut everything down when I found texts I shouldn't have seen, the part of me that cut me off from sex for so long.

What I knew about Q who had my heart is that he wasn't tougher than me, he wasn't going to be my guardian against the world, and he couldn't save me. I wanted to be with him because everything about him, from his body to his mind to his damage, turned me on – not because I thought he could protect me.

I didn't yet know that, weeks from then, I'd meet Paula, tentative and shy, from a long-haul flight. That she would, almost immediately, win us all over. That she'd get Ben on a regular schedule so he had CJ every Saturday and she'd guide him to accepting that he could no longer live in a different city from his daughter. She'd do CJ's hair and bake with her, and she and I would see together the films Ben had no interest in. I didn't yet know that, unlike me, she wasn't scared of him – not at all – and it was one of the things he loved her for.

I saw how he calmed down when he knew he wasn't feared. That I'd wish in my deepest bones for them to stay together – that I'd start to count off the days waiting for him to ask her to marry him until, finally, he did. That, if she'd been conjured – my former fan-turned-ex-husband's fiancée – having been drawn to our orbit by a book I once wrote, it wasn't to usurp or terrorise, as goes the third act of eighties movies. The twist ending was she was there to make my life easier.

You know who slid into Ben's DMs?

An actual angel.

But I don't think I conjured Paula – who speaks three languages fluently and loves Wong Kar Wai movies and has a stack of Camille Paglia and Elif Batuman books on the go. I think she is very much her own person with a vast future ahead of her. I like her so much not only because she is so likeable, but also, significantly, because I like myself now.

All things can happen with time. You just have to stay alive to see them. There are myriad small but perfectly formed miracles that you'll never get to witness without ageing. It's a fair trade-off. If I had stayed with Ben, almost a decade my senior, I'd always have been 'younger'. It truly felt like a valid reason to stay. Because I was scared. My whole body, now shaking with erotic sensation, vibrated with fear back then.

I accept that, from all corners, my non-nuclear family's parameters are non-normal. There is an utter disregard for boundaries – and it *is* weird, but it's not cruel. It's less peculiar than chewing and spitting bags of sweets into a rubbish bin while your husband wanders in and out of the room. So she wrote Ben a letter on Facebook after being a fan of my memoir? Guess what? She's not done anything I wouldn't at her age.

But I hadn't met Paula yet. I only knew my bound arms were aching from the ties of the Gucci scarf. And, as the last streaks of pink melted out of the sky, the musician came all over me. I was bioluminescent in the dark.

There's been great pain in my life over the disconnect between how things are in my head and how they are when they become real. But after the long celibacy, I now found I had the power to conjure sexual encounters exactly the way they were in my fantasies.

What I loved and still love about that night was that it was everything that could ever be beautiful in a relationship, edited all the way down. I felt safe and free. No one was harmed. No one did harm. Two humans transformed into animals, and then back again by daylight. And for the first time, I can remember not carrying deep sadness about returning to earth after such a crazy high.

Q was busy self-actualising that weekend, which is precisely the right thing to do not only in your twenties, but also in your forties. And that's why I felt he would understand what I was doing, too, tied to the staircase by a stranger I'd never see again. I was transforming. I was being a slut and a whore and all that good stuff, but I was transfiguring, too.

I couldn't have done any of it without all those years of quiet. I cannot say which meant more to me, only that celibacy and sex wrap around each other like lovers. They come at the same time, looking into each other's eyes. I can see this is unreadable pornography for some – for many, maybe – but it meant something to me, that one-night stand. It meant I was obliterated and that I was alive, still, two decades after a suicide bid. Alive in the most primal way – more alive than I'd ever been.

I know that sex or no sex, I'll continue to live more deeply until it starts to wind the other way and I have to live more lightly because the choice is out of my hands. I am autumn now, dazzled by my own colours, but, eventually, I will be winter.

The song on my playlist he first messaged me about, the one he thought made me cool as fuck? 'Tusk' by Fleetwood Mac. That album was a big failure compared to *Rumours*. But. It does have the line: 'Don't say that you love me. Just tell me that you want me' – against a tune so percussive, so convincing, the same way New York's numbered streets always encouraged me to keep walking.

My plan had been to let this new boy fuck the crazy out of me so I could go back to Q without holding my breath for each text and muting WhatsApp messages that I'd then retrieve from the bin to eat. Though I found him difficult, diffident and confusing, he also fascinated me – maybe we might end up boyfriend and girlfriend. Maybe that wouldn't be possible.

But this boy, this one in my flat, I wasn't scared of this boy: I loved him that night, that night as I fell asleep in his arms, *Wildflowers* playing, I felt I loved him as much as I'd loved my husband. My text and my subtext had equal voice.

See, this time you don't have to choose each other. You don't have to find out down the line you chose wrong, or watch helplessly as it falls apart. You never have to re-member how passionate you were for each other and how far apart you now are in the bed. You can just *obliterate* each other, clean yourself with the Gucci scarf and then, very gently, with the morning light moving across the street, walk him to the underground, kiss him, watch him descend. And with the sky still above you and the pavement still beneath you, you can just let go . . .

I couldn't have directed that night, dared to have set the scenes and asked for them – positioned these men in the places I wanted them to be with the lighting I saw in my head and the soundtrack that suited the light – if I had not directed my movie that nobody saw. My ex-husband helped me to do that. There is only one physical sensation I have as strong as an orgasm. My ex-husband makes me laugh hysterically until I am on my hands and knees, clawing for air, saying, 'Please, Ben, please.' This makes him very happy. You could say we have no business bringing each other this pleasure after all the pain we have caused. But we can't help it. It's just chemistry.

In the top-floor flat that gave me my life back, my renter was about to arrive and everything I own was gone. The removal men didn't notice me at all, because I was a woman in my forties and I hadn't turned my light on for them. I glanced beyond them, at the spiral staircase, as I exited.

If I did go back to my neighbourhood in California, if I could go back, all the things I loved are gone. The Chateau Marmont Hotel has closed down – it is rumoured, will become apartments or a members' club. Its fate is currently unclear, only that it won't be what it was. Divorce is a kind of gentrification. Reverse gentrification, too, because of the pandemic and lockdowns. Along the five blocks I'd walk from my house to my Pilates teacher Audrey's studio, all of our favourites – the cafés, the vintage T-shirt store, the dance studio – have gone out of business – are boarded over, graffitied and littered with broken glass. It feels like divorce because it means nothing and everything to the situation that I knew what was once there. How vibrant and how much joy we had there. And how I knew those spaces inside out.

Ben can see full well I've stopped being Starship and turned back into Jefferson Airplane. He didn't make it happen. I did. But he can see it. What only I know is that the reason I loved *Surrealistic Pillow* so much in the first place is because it's one of my mum's favourite records. On her deathbed, if I get to be there, I would say, 'I love you, but I also had a *blast* with you! I had such a good time. I enjoyed you so, so much. And, hey: Mario Cuomo's son got done for sexual harassment and he never got to be president. But Biden did.'

I said 'Love Me Like a Woman' had a word super-imposed over a word, a want over a truth. The musician didn't know I didn't tell Ben what I really wanted when we first met, how I'd said, 'I don't want to be your girl-friend.' Or at the end when I told him I could live with there being other women. Or how I'd pretended to the producer in Tuscany that the ring he gave me meant nothing to me when it meant a lot. That boy stopped and listened and said, 'Yes, what you noticed in the song was correct and yes, what an amazing thing.' To be seen, to have witnesses, is the most you can ask. They don't have to stay forever. They can stay a decade or year or six months or three months or one night, and what they saw with you will not go away just because they have.

It was real: the LA mountains. The walks with no pavement. The baby. The love so great you got married. The pain so intolerable you got divorced. The reservoir full and the reservoir drained. The reality-show host with the nuclear codes. Children in cages changing nappies of toddlers. The people who breached the US Capitol. The strange young man who took off your underwear with his teeth. George Michael and Tom Petty, and the songs that are so alive and the creators who are dead and never coming back. The fireworks over North London.

Lockdown. The metal of the staircase against your shoulder blades, the softness of the scarf against your wrists. How much your daughter hates you going out one night a week. How much you'll miss your mother when she's gone. How badly you've failed, holding the gaze of the times you got it right.

It was real. It was really real. And you don't have to be afraid any more.

Epilogue

Before I decide to sleep with someone else, to distract me from my obsession with Q, I find myself pacing around my bedroom.

By my bedside is a biography of Shakespeare and Company – the oldest bookstore in Paris and the scene of our final crime, where my husband and I tried to touch but, instead, pulled apart forever. Inside it I find a heart card with a tender inscription, reminding me of all the good we've had in all our ferocity, and I remember him giving it to me when we had filed for divorce but it had yet to come through.

My stomach doesn't drop any more at the sight of a book inscription in Ben's lost little boy handwriting. When I find one of the three copies he bought of Nile Rodger's autobiography because he was convinced they'd only increase in value, I no longer scoff but feel warm. Then a weird thing happens.

It's past midnight. I've never cried to him before about someone who is not him.

In truth, I've come to the point where I'm crying so hard, I can't get the words out.

'Emmy? Emmy? I'm calling you back on video. I want to see your face.'

He calls me back. I don't need to look pretty for him any more. Not any more.

'What happened?' he asks, his round blue eyes seeming to pull his freckles closer like a blanket.

'All I do, every hour of the day, is think about fucking Q. I was holding on to the dishwasher, thinking about getting railed. And our kid left home!'

'It's fine.'

'It's not fine to be daydreaming about sex so intensely that our seven-year-old walks out of the house without me knowing!'

'Well, I'm gonna talk to her. She can't do that.'

I wipe my snot.

'Have you seen a 27-year-old's body?'

'Yes.'

'Well I haven't, because I was always with older men. His body is too beautiful for my eyes and . . .' I'm *sobbing*. 'That is all that I'm equipped with.' This is a Peter Cook line handed down from my parents.

'Fozzy . . .'

But he lets me talk over him.

'And . . . I don't understand what he wants from me. He's got this unusually full life. He doesn't have space for me, but he keeps on sending all these great songs all of the time, into the ether. Am I the ether?'

Now he stops me.

'Have a breath. You're not the ether. You're Emma fuckin' Forrest.'

It takes me aback to hear him say my name. Not 'Fozzy' or 'Mum'. Not infantilised or maternalised. But actually . . . me. It makes me calm down.

'I feel crazy since I started having sex again. Like my nervous system is in a civil war with my lust.'

'I knew this would happen. I knew it. Here's what you do: fuck him a few more times and you will stop feeling so crazy. Hang up, call him up, tell him, "Q, I need you to get over here and fuck me."'

'I think – I think that may seem a bit frightening. I don't want to send him away.'

'Fine. Give me his number, I'll do it. I'll call him up and say: "Listen, cunt. Go over there while my kid's asleep and fuck my ex-wife."'

'I think, I'm not sure, but that also may strike him as scary.'

But I start to laugh and once I do, I notice I'm not crying any more.

In many ways my marriage, like my film, failed. Except, despite it all, that film was my cut. It didn't stay on screens more than a few days. But what was there, in the moments it was on screen, was mine. Ben was the one who told me to approach it as if I may never be given another chance.

Would you go through all that, the fights about money that you'll each go to your grave feeling you were right about? All that romantic shame and humiliation, heartbreak – if it meant that there is someone who genuinely loves you, who you genuinely love, who can talk you down past midnight?

He can hear that, too, and begins to change the subject. I am half listening, swooning and wanting to huff the tights from my first time with Q that I couldn't bring myself to wash. I can't, in good conscience, say that a presidential term of celibacy means my lessons have been learned. But I know that if I can't always fix them, I can at least see them. That is something new.

'Hey, Foz. I watched the rest of *Once Upon a Time in Hollywood*.'

'Yeah? What did you think of it?'

'Oh, Emmy, I think it's very beautiful.'

'It is.'

And we both agree: neither of us knew the film would end that way.

Acknowledgements

To my literary agent, Felicity Rubinstein: thank you for your decades-long wisdom and friendship. You are the best.

To Elinor Burns at Casarotto Ramsay & Associates: it's also many years we've travelled together, and I'm so grateful you're still by and on my side. Thank you to Gabriel, Catherine, Nicholas and Jenne for stepping up when you selfishly had a baby.

Lettice Franklin: this is my seventh book, but my first with you. You feel indispensable to what I've been trying to get across (for twenty years). This book was half as good before you cast your eye over it.

Thank you Kim Witherspoon, for so many years of support.

Robert Montgomery: I am still pinching myself that an artist whose work brought me such comfort as I wrote this book ended up agreeing to make the cover.

Debra Diez: thank you for your constant kindness and for just making life easier.

My sister, Lisa: I am pleased you are the first sister on Earth who will never die and will always be there with me, until the day we hold hands and disintegrate at the same perfect moment.

To my parents, Judy and Jeffrey (always, even when it's the first one I do not want them to read).

I received valuable early reads of the manuscript from Shana Feste, Kelly Marcel, Shannon Murphy, Millie Warner and Minnie Driver. Thank you all so much.

Thank you to Lisa Taddeo, reading with such generosity the bits and pieces of a virtual stranger as they arrived.

Hadley Freeman and Jess Cartner-Morley were the first readers of *The Guardian* essay from which this memoir was expanded. Their advice to go ahead and publish it meant the world. Thank you Melissa Denes for commissioning it.

Thank you, Jemima Kirke, for some things, and Lola Kirke for different things. You each have a part of my heart.

Susie Ember is a real 'without whom', as are Indira Varma, Eliza Mishcon, Aoife and Phil Hassett, and Daniela Dessa.

SB and Maysan, thank you for The Chain – I love you.

Thank you, so very much, Lucia.

Jasmine Lee-Jones: couldn't have passed the magic keys to a writer worthier than you.

At Orion, my thanks to Virginia Woolstencroft, Lynsey Sutherland, Steve Marking, Jenny Lord, Clarissa Sutherland, Ellie Freedman and Paul Stark.

Thank you to Claire Dean for copy-editing, and to Felicity Price at Reviewed and Cleared.

Thank you Elisa Christophe at Epilogue.

Holding together the non-nuclear family:

Thank you Sophia Wright-Mendelsohn and Leah Wright.

Thank you Grandpa Fred and Red Nana.

Thank you, most of all, to CJ, for putting so much joy inside my tears.

Thank you Q, I'm so glad it was you.

Thank you, finally, to Ben: you're a badass, if you didn't know. Thank you Paula, who I trust with my kid and who trusted me with my words. You've both allowed me to tell our story my way, and I won't forget it.

Text Credits